THREAT FORECASTING

THREAT FORECASTING

Leveraging Big Data for Predictive Analysis

JOHN PIRC
DAVID DESANTO
IAIN DAVISON
WILL GRAGIDO

AMSTERDAM • BOSTON • HEIDELBERG • LONDON
NEW YORK • OXFORD • PARIS • SAN DIEGO
SAN FRANCISCO • SINGAPORE • SYDNEY • TOKYO

Syngress is an Imprint of Elsevier

SYNGRESS

Syngress is an imprint of Elsevier
50 Hampshire Street, 5th Floor, Cambridge, MA 02139, USA

Library of Congress Cataloging-in-Publication Data
A catalog record for this book is available from the Library of Congress

British Library Cataloguing-in-Publication Data
A catalogue record for this book is available from the British Library

ISBN: 978-0-12-800006-9

For information on all Syngress publications
visit our website at https://www.elsevier.com/

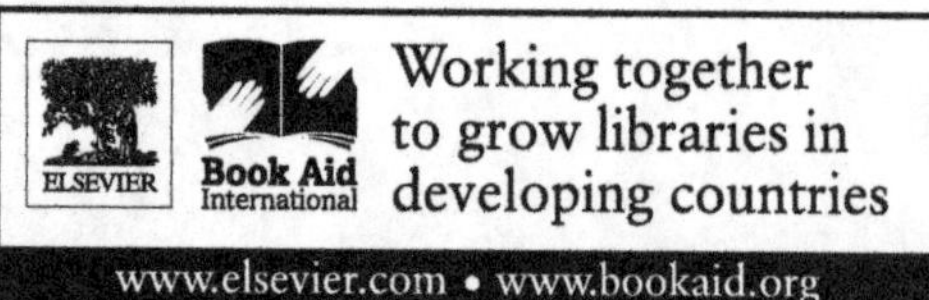

Publisher: Todd Green
Acquisition Editor: Chris Katsaropoulos
Editorial Project Manager: Anna Valutkevich
Production Project Manager: Punithavathy Govindaradjane
Designer: Mark Rogers

Typeset by SPi Global, India

CONTENTS

ABOUT THE AUTHORS

John Pirc has more than 19 years of experience in Security R&D, worldwide security product management, marketing, testing, forensics, consulting, and critical infrastructure architecting and deployment. Additionally, John is an advisor to HP's CISO on Cyber Security and has lectured at the US Naval Post Graduate School.

John extensive expertise in the security field stems from past work experience with the US Intelligence Community, as Chief Technology Officer at CSG LTD, Product Manager at Cisco, Product Line Executive for all security products at IBM Internet Security Systems, Director at McAfee's Network Defense Business Unit, Director of Product Management at HP Enterprise Security Products, Chief Technology Officer at NSS Labs, Co-Founder and Chief Strategy Officer at Bricata, LLC and, most recently as Director of Security Solutions for Forsythe Technology.

In addition to a BBA from the University of Texas, John also holds the NSA-IAM and CEH certifications. He has been named security thought leader from SANS Institute and speaks at top tier security conferences worldwide and has been published in Time Magazine, Bloomberg, CNN and other tier 1 media outlets.

David DeSanto is a network security professional with over 15 years of security research, security testing, software development and product strategy experience. He is a strong technical leader with a firm understanding of TCP/IP, software development experience, including automation frameworks, and a deep knowledge in securing the enterprise network.

David is the Director, Products and Threat Research for Spirent Communications where he drives product strategy for all application security testing solutions. He also manages the security engineering team responsible for the research, development and validation of new security attacks (i.e., exploits, malware, DDoS attacks) as well as development of all engine components that support them. Prior to Spirent, David's career included roles at the industry's top security research and testing labs, where his expertise guided these organizations in creating industry-leading security tests and solutions for enterprises, services providers and network equipment vendors.

David holds a Master of Science in Cybersecurity from New York University School of Engineering and Bachelor of Science in Computer Science from Millersville University. He is a frequent speaker at major international conferences on topics including threat intelligence, cloud security, GNSS security issues and the impacts of SSL decryption on today's next generation security products.

Iain Davison has over 16 years of security experience, with many skills ranging from penetration testing to creating and building intrusion prevention devices. This includes knowledge of programming languages, scripting, and compiling software. In his last position, Iain performed network architecture, hardware design, software design, and implementation.

He currently lives in Clinton, MD, with his wife Laura and two kids Shaun age 6 and Emma age 1; he also has a dog and a cat. Iain enjoys creating home automation devices from raspberry pi kits along with home media and simple robotics.

Along with his experience in the cyber-security industry, Iain has also written a book with a few of colleagues on threat forecasting, it will be published in the second quarter of this year. The book discusses some techniques used to gather intelligence, the importance of all data not just the obvious. Looking at data from a different perspective, something other than the norm.

Now that he is on the Exabeam team, he may be willing to write yet another book based around UBA and all the things it can do in the enterprise.

Will Gragido possesses over 21 years of information security experience. A former United States Marine, Mr. Gragido began his career in the data communications information security and intelligence communities. After USMC, Mr. Gragido worked within several information security consultancy roles performing and leading red teaming, penetration testing, incident response, security assessments, ethical hacking, malware analysis and risk management program development. Mr. Gragido has worked with a variety of industry leading research organizations including International Network Services, Internet Security Systems/IBM Internet Security Systems X-Force, Damballa, Cassandra Security, HP DVLabs, RSA NetWitness, and now Digital Shadows. Will has deep expertise and knowledge in operations, analysis, management, professional services and consultancy, pre-sales/architecture and has a strong desire to see the industry mature, and enterprises and individuals become more secure. Will holds a CISSP and has accreditations with the National Security Agency's Information Security Assessment Methodology (IAM) and Information Security Evaluation Methodology (IEM). Mr. Gragido is a graduate of DePaul University and is currently in graduate school. An internationally sought after speaker, Will is the co-author of *Cybercrime and Espionage: An Analysis of Subversive Multi-Vector Threats* and *Blackhatonomics: An Inside Look At The Economics of Cybercrime.*

FOREWORD

"Some things are so unexpected that no one is prepared for them."

–Leo Rosten in *Rome Wasn't Burned in a Day*

For the last decade, I've been engaged in helping customers and vendors mitigate the risks of a cyberattack. If there is one thing I've learned, it's that the adversary is dynamic, fast moving, ever changing and that their targets are usually unprepared.

How do you prepare for a threat and adversary so dynamic and innovative? What can we learn from the adversary? How can we intersect with where the adversary is headed? Most notably, how we can use the strategies that are employed by the adversary to change our posture from one of viewing the threat in the rear view mirror to a more balanced, proactive stance. This is the crux of *Threat Forecasting*.

I have spent the last 30+ years engaged with IT executives in various leadership roles in the computing, networking and information security industry. I had the benefit of cutting my teeth in the IT industry as a young manager during the early days of networking working at 3Com Corporation for, among others, Robert Metcalfe, one of the principal inventors of Ethernet. That experience served as a launching pad for my departure from 3Com. I engaged in leadership roles in an early stage database analytic company founded and lead by the likes of Brad Silverberg and Adam Bosworth. Brad was the Microsoft executive responsible for the Windows platform. Adam Bosworth is a recognized innovator with a career arc that includes his principle role as the creator of XMS while at Microsoft, a senior executive at Google as the VP of Product Management, and now the EVP at Salesforce.com responsible for the development of their next generation platform for IoT and Cloud.

During the first decade of my career, I matured professionally inside the tornado of the emergence of the personal computer. My time at 3Com introduced me to the power of the network and Metcalfe's Law.

Metcalfe's law states that the value of a telecommunications network is proportional to the square of the number of connected users of the system (n^2).

The fundamental premise of Metcalfe's law is the value of the network grows geometrically as the number of users grows.

The authors of *Threat Forecasting* apply this same principle to the value of intelligent threat exchange. The authors explore how your organization can benefit from intelligent analysis of real-time threat information. Just as Metcalfe's law describes the benefit of the computer network, so too do the authors educate us about the benefit of leveraging external and internal sources of Indicators of Interest (IOI), Indicators of Attack (IOA) and Indicators of Compromise (IOC).

As I rode the wave of the emergence of the personal computer and networking, I was exposed to the inherent tension between the economic advantages of client-server, Web 1.0 and Web 2.0 architectures and the inherent challenges of maintaining security and control of the network and its sensitive data.

For the last decade, I have been deeply engaged in IT security. Having helped countless organizations implement next generation computing products and architectures. During this journey I have been continuously confronted with the inherent challenges associated with securing customer networks. That journey led me to a leadership role as the President of TippingPoint technologies, an early leader in network Intrusion Prevention Systems (IPS). TippingPoint was later acquired by 3Com, which was then acquired by Hewlett Packard Corporation. HP acquired ArcSight, the leading SIEM provider, and Fortify, the leading application security product at the time. While at HP I briefly led the product organization for the newly created Enterprise Security Products organization and ultimately was responsible for our global enterprise security product go-to-market.

My time at HP gave me a comprehensive view of what it means to provide defense-in-depth from the network, to the application, to the end system and data. After 18 months at HP I left to join Vormetric Data Security as its current President and CEO. As I write this forward, Vormetric is in the process of being acquired by Thales S.A., a leader in global defense and electronic systems. Their e-Security group is a leader in payment processing and general-purpose encryption hardware security modules (HSMs). The vast majority of payment transactions our touched by Thales systems each and every day. I will serve as the CEO of its global data security business unit, Thales e-Security.

I was drawn to Threat Forecasting based on my many years of experience of being engaged with the authors. I have had the pleasure of working directly with the authors at TippingPoint, HP and beyond. Their experience in working with the intelligence community as subject matter experts used to dissecting high-profile breaches and as designers and developers of products uniquely qualifies them to speak to the benefit of Threat Forecasting.

John Pirc, David DeSanto, Iain Davison and Will Gragido bring decades of combined experience with a unique mix of security product development, strategy, engineering, testing, incident response and much more. This combined expertise and the coaching they have received from industry leaders throughout their careers, has provided them with the insight and drive to push the security industry to the next level.

"My interest is in the future because I am going to spend the rest of my life there."

–C.F. Kettering

The authors are uniquely qualified to appreciate the impact of and challenges involved in protecting us against cyber-attacks and why this remains one of the greatest challenges of our increasingly connected world.

Why Threat Forecasting is Relevant

The pace of change in our connected world is accelerating. All one has to do is reflect on the recent spate of high-profile breaches and the commensurate brand and financial damage incurred to appreciate the industry needs a new approach. Yesterday's tools and yesterday's thinking simply no longer apply. The challenge is exacerbated with the proliferation of Internet of Things (IoT) devices, autonomous vehicles and the need for an increased level of trust between applications and devices in our more connected world.

What You Will Learn and How You Will Benefit

"The journey of a thousand miles begins with one step."

–Lao Tzu, Chinese Philosopher

I started this forward by citing the benefits attributed to the network effect of Metcalfe's Law. Metcalfe's Law and the network effect are a model and a metaphor for the advantages of communities of interest, which are at the crux of the power of Threat Forecasting.

If you are a *security practitioner,* you will gain guidance and a roadmap to help you begin the journey. The authors explain the legacy of threat reporting, and compare and contrast threat reporting with threat forecasting. You will be given a checklist of available tools, both open source and commercial, to help you understand the design of a security architecture that is threat forecast enabled.

If you are an *IT or security executive* (Chief Information Security Officer), you will benefit from an education about the learning from recent high-profile data breaches. You will gain a greater appreciation of the efficacy of existing security solutions deployed in your network. You will gain insight into the key nomenclature in a way that is practical and easily consumable, thereby helping you engage in thoughtful dialog with your risk and security teams.

The authors present relevant, practical data that will help you enlist the support of your colleagues, and executive management and board, to build consensus around a journey to engage in a threat forecasting initiative. Of particular relevance is an explanation of the power of communities of interest. You will learn the benefits of participating in a threat-sharing community of interest. You will learn the opportunities and risks associated with participation. You'll learn how best to prepare your organization and existing information security infrastructure to maximize the value of the near real-time information gleaned from participation in, or subscription to, community of interest threat data.

Alan Kessler
President and CEO, Vormetric Data Security

PREFACE

Man has endeavored to see beyond his circumstances since time immemorial. He has developed and adopted a vast and wide array of esoteric beliefs and rituals, which, over time, aided him to one degree or another in making decisions that would have ramifications on individuals, communities, populations, and empires. Throughout history, man's desire to know and understand the future has encouraged him to strive toward greater and greater heights; heights that could only be reached by dismissing the esoteric in favor of the scientific. Today, man continues to forecast and predict outcomes, only now instead of looking into the mists or at the bones, man looks at evidence; at math and contemplates probability based on a variety of factors all of which can be explained through science and articulated in such a way that the everyone can understand. This book deals with an area that is emerging. It is growing and developing, and is being nurtured by a portion of the Information Security industry, that in some ways is at a pivot point, where it is destined to move from the modern equivalent of esotericism to the new reality. In this book the concept of threat forecasting and predictive analysis is introduced to the reader in a manner that is easy to understand and digestible. It is delivered in 10 chapters all of which have been written and contributed to by the industry's leading subject matter experts with combined experience that can be measured in decades. This book will challenge some to look beyond the mist and embrace the scientific; the tangible. It will encourage the reader to think differently with respect to navigating and negotiating today's threats, threat forecasting, security intelligence and the threat landscape itself.

Book Organization and Structure

During the following ten chapters the reader will be exposed to concepts and ideas that they may have considered but never employed or to those that are entirely new. Each chapter offers a unique view of our experiences and thoughts. The book is broken down in the following manner:

Chapter 1: *Navigating Today's Threat Landscape*—We start by discussing the issues within today's threat landscape and show the need for a better solution. A high-level discussion around industry regulations will help set the tone for why threat forecasting is needed. We finish this chapter by challenging today's information assurance practices.

Chapter 2: *Threat Forecasting*—We discuss the foundations of threat forecasting and compare patterns used to other types of forecasting you may be familiar with. This chapter will also lay some of the foundations for future chapters, including a discussion around big data and its importance within threat forecasting.

Chapter 3: *Security Intelligence*—We will introduce you to security intelligence and help structure what a security intelligence platform should look like for your organization. This chapter will also discuss key performance indicators that are commonly associated with security intelligence.

Chapter 4: *Identifying Knowledge Elements*—We define key terms that may be new to the reader including Indicators of Compromise (IOCs) and Indicators of Interest (IOIs). We help identify some issues when collecting knowledge elements and help provide guidance on how to address them to get the best data possible for knowledge sharing and threat modeling.

Chapter 5: *Knowledge Sharing and Community Support*—The advantages and disadvantages to sharing knowledge elements are discussed and we reassure the reader that it is best to share and gain knowledge than be left in the dark. We outline several popular community threat intelligence feeds and how to become active within the threat intelligence community.

Chapter 6: *Data Visualization*—We use this chapter to outline the different ways to visualize your data for analysis and simulation. Three-dimensional graphs are reviewed and comparisons are drawn to other industries that leverage similar technologies. Visualization is a key component on the road to threat forecasting.

Chapter 7: *Data Simulation*—In this chapter we discuss several topics as they relate to data simulation. These include comparisons between simulation and emulation, the importance of dealing with knowledge elements (discussed in Chapter 4) and the types of engines available today. Future topics are discussed including leveraging quantum computing for faster data results.

Chapter 8: *Kill Chain Modeling*—We define kill chain modeling and discuss how it associates with threat forecasting. We dissect the individual components to help you better understand its necessity within this type of threat modeling. We discuss the role of big data as well as the tools available today to assist with kill chain modeling.

Chapter 9: *Connecting The Dots*—We bring together all the individual topics discussed throughout the book and show how not paying attention to the current landscape can impact your organization. Real-world examples are used to show how threat forecasting can play an integral part in protecting organizations within all industry verticals. This chapter serves as a call to action to begin applying the techniques that can improve your organization's security practices and procedures.

Chapter 10: *The Road Ahead*—In our final chapter, we discuss our opinions for the future of both threat forecasting as well as the Information Security as a whole. Our diverse background provides you with four unique views on how several key issues within the cyber security industry, as well as a unique view on the challenges that lie ahead for organizations from all industry verticals.

Closing Thoughts

Our collaboration and dedication to bringing to the market the most comprehensive book on this subject is evident and of value to anyone who picks it up. To the reader, we wish that you gain knowledge and insights into the topic of threat forecasting and predictive analysis. It is our hope that you will find this book novel, informative and educational, as it is our belief that it is one of the earliest published works on this subject. This is the combined work of four information security professionals located across three of the four time zones of the United States and was also written while the authors were traveling to various events, including speaking at international conferences, attending customer security consulting engagements and visiting our international offices. We hope you find this book to be a good travel companion on the road to threat forecasting and predictive analysis, as it was on its way from idea to inception.

ACKNOWLEDGMENTS

The journey of a thousand miles begins with one step

Lao Tzu

I want to dedicate this book to my Lord and Savior Jesus Christ, my wife, kids, and my mom (Judy Pirc)...I love you all. After writing two books, I didn't think I would ever do a third. I've had the pleasure to be involved in both early stage startups and well-established high-tech security companies. I've been honored to have influenced various security products working with some very strong teams. The experience has provided me with many opportunities to experience what works and frankly what doesn't. To some this concept of Threat Forecasting that I envisioned almost 4 years ago, some of the parts of which might be considered mainstream/bleeding edge security products and services, today might appear an impossible or a crazy idea.

On this journey, I quickly realized that I couldn't take on this project by myself and needed some of the best minds, with expertise in threat intelligence, hardware design, data science, data modeling, virtualization, SaaS, and product development; people whom I trusted to participate, to add to the project and to challenge me. I decided to involve David DeSanto, Iain Davison, and Will Gragido all of whom I trust and respect, as they are not afraid of giving brutally honest feedback and it doesn't hurt that they are close friends. After I briefed them on the original concept...let's say some of my theories were challenged and they pushed me to a level of innovation that I had thought was beyond my capabilities. I'm very proud of their contributions and thought leadership in Threat Forecasting.

Lastly, I want to thank a few people that have been instrumental in my career, Stephen Northcutt, Bob Bigman, John Webster, John Watkins, Greg Adams, Alan Kessler, Heath Peyton, John Lawrence, Ernest Rocha, Frank Oakes, Chris Morales, Dan Holden, Daniel J. Molina, Dan Seeley, Brendan Laws, Craig Lawson, Steve MacDonald, Scott Lupfer, Jacque Kernot, Brian Reed, Jason Lamar, Rees Johnson, Vik Phatak, Bob Walder, ReseAnne Sims, Kris Lamb, Eric York, David Poarch, Chris Becker, Lance Grover, Rich Raines, Andria Green, Chad Randolph, Mark Dowd, George V. Hulme, Ofir Zelnik, Donovan Kolbly, Gary Steely, Dillon Beresford, Ragy Magdy, Melanie Kesler Coppen, Mark Finke, Melinda

Fieldus, John Cardani-Trollinger, Chris Jobe, Enrique Rangel, Nick Selby, Gunter Ollman, Hillary Noye, Michael Jones, Thomas Skybakmoen, Jon Amato, Dave Barron, Barret Sellers, Toshikazu Murata, Adam Hils, Rafal Los, Elisa Contreras Lippincott, Nelson Brito, Chris Thomas, Dana Torgersen, Richard Stiennon, Jason Burn, Sean Brown, Youssef El Malty, Daniel Powers, Rohit Dhamankar, Matt Wong, Mark Scianna, Tom Cross, Stefan Korsbacken, Denis Batrankov, Steve Spring, Julian McBride, Jason Hilling, Sumeet Gohri, Arun George, Russ Meyers, Val Rahmani, Scott Paisley, Munawar Hossain, Brent Fowler, Jerry Fraizer, Ralph Richardson, Stephen Driggers, and Sanjay Raja. There are many more…but thank you for investing in me!

John Pirc

First and foremost, I want to thank Liz, my wife and best friend. Thank you for your unconditional love and unwavering support. I jumped into this project while in the middle of my Master of Science degree at NYU, which meant only your constant support (and a lot of caffeine) could make this a reality. This book could not have happened without you! Thank you for supporting my crazy ideas and being there to help me through the difficult times. I look forward to our continued journey together. Next, I would like to thank John for inviting me onto this project as well as Will and Iain for coming along for the ride. We have put together something to be proud of. Our combined experiences make for a very unique perspective on Threat Forecasting. Next, I would like to thank the people throughout my career who have helped me. You have each played a role in getting me to where I am today and I thank you for constantly challenging me. Finally, I would like to thank you the reader. This book was written for those seeking new knowledge to better understand today and tomorrow's threat landscape to best secure their organization. St. Francis of Assisi said "Start by doing what's necessary; then do what's possible; and suddenly you are doing the impossible." I hope you find the knowledge you seek so that the impossible begins to become possible for you and your team.

David DeSanto

I would like to also dedicate my parts of the book to my wife Laura and my kids Shaun and Emma. Thank you for supporting me during this project.

Iain Davison

When I sat down to write this acknowledgment my first instinct was to begin by thanking those closest to me for their support and encouragement throughout the process. And though there will be some of that—thanking some key folks who supported my co-authors and me during the creative process—this will not be a dedication. This is an acknowledgment; this is an expression of gratitude and appreciation to those who played a key role in making this book a reality. I'd like to first acknowledge my wife, Tracy Gragido, and our kids. Their willingness to "share" me with my co-authors on nights and weekends made this process much easier than it would have been were that not the case. I'd also like to acknowledge my co-authors: John, David, and Iain. Thank you guys for allowing me to join you on this journey into the unknown. We set out to write a book on a topic that is nascent, emerging, and we did just that. Our ideas and thoughts (hopefully) will aid in spurring on new thought leaders and visionaries, for after all, as Arthur O'Shaughnessy said, "...we are the music makers, we are the dreamers of dreams..." I'd also like to acknowledge our team at Syngress, specifically Anna, for her patience and help along the way. Last but not least, I'd like to acknowledge you, the reader, for taking the time to peruse all the books on this subject and selecting this one to add to your reading list or collection. It is my sincere hope that it aids you in finding the answers you seek.

Will Gragido

1

NAVIGATING TODAY'S THREAT LANDSCAPE

Introduction

Today's threat landscape is often compared to a high stakes game of whac-a-mole: just as security professionals focus on thwarting one mole-like threat, others are already popping up. Security threats emerge at a dizzying speed and security professionals are often left reeling as the threat landscape changes around them. A vital tool in understanding these changes has been historical threat reporting. Historical threat reports summarize events related to security threats over a fixed period of time. There are legions of historical threat reports available; a Google search for "cyber security threat report" yields over three million results. These reports may cover general cyber security threats or specific focus areas (e.g., web-based applications). There are quarterly threat reports and annual threat reports, but all historical threat reports reflect backwards.

Historical threat reports have the valuable attribute of mapping out the threat landscape as it appeared in the past. And, although many historical threat reports attempt to predict future trends and shifts, they provide only limited visibility into the threat landscapes of today and tomorrow. To combat the threats of today and predict the threats of tomorrow, enterprises need to view their security infrastructure, products and data collection in a different way. Instead of reporting after the fact, threat forecasting looks to prevent security incidents and data breaches before they happen. The exploration of threat forecasting as laid out in this book will give organizations the tools needed to protect themselves in an ever evolving threat landscape. By adopting a

Threat Forecasting. http://dx.doi.org/10.1016/B978-0-12-800006-9.00001-X

policy of threat forecasting, security professionals can stop playing whac-a-mole and begin to know where the next threat is likely to come from.

Why Threat Forecasting

No organization is impervious to security failures. By adopting a systematic approach to threat forecasting, your organization can not only improve your defenses against today's threats, but also form reasonable predictions about the threats of tomorrow. Although, it is true that no threat forecasting approach will be able to predict and stop attacks 100% of the time, when it is carried out correctly and consistently, threat forecasting will increase your organizational efficacy in detecting and preventing attacks. The side effect of preventing attacks is saving your company time, money and the embarrassment of a public data breach.

Threat forecasting allows you to apply real-world threat intelligence to the data collected within your organization to identify patterns or trends "in-the-wild" (i.e., currently active on the Internet) that may impact your organization. Threat forecasting enables your organization to:

- identify knowledge elements within your data for collection for tracking/reporting (refer to Chapter 4—Identifying Knowledge Elements)
- subscribe to threat intelligence feeds to get a holistic view of the greater threat landscape (refer to Chapter 5—Knowledge Sharing and Community Support)
- combine all datasets together and use identified trends to determine high-risk elements and provide protection to vulnerable areas prior to attack/breach (refer to Chapter 6—Data Visualization and Chapter 7—Data Simulation).

Please refer to Chapter 2—Threat Forecasting for more information.

The Effects of a Data Breach

Data breaches are becoming part of our daily lives. Adversaries are better organized than ever and they are likely targeting your company's data. This is not a scare tactic or a way to encourage you to go out and buy a bunch of security equipment. The message we want to convey is that no one is immune and data breaches are almost an inevitable occurrence in today's threat landscape. Malicious threat actors are attacking all industries and are targeting both smaller startups and giant multinational corporations. As a consequence of these malicious activities, the Incident Response (IR) market has exploded in recent years. By 2017, the IR market is expected to grow into a $14 billion industry.[1]

With costs both tangible and intangible rapidly accumulating in the wake of a data breach, there's no doubt a data breach will cost your organization big bucks. A Ponemon Institute study found that not only have cyber-attacks increased in frequency in recent years but also it is becoming more expensive to address them, with the average data breach costing companies in the study $3.8 million.[2] When remedying a data breach your organization will incur two types of costs: direct and indirect. Direct costs include contracting outside forensic or IR experts, outsourcing customer hotline support, notifying customers (both digitally as well as via mail), providing credit monitoring subscriptions for customers and offering free or discounted future products and services. Although indirect costs can be more difficult to quantify, these costs include internal investigations and communication, customer attrition and weakened customer acquisition rates. Indirect costs represent the harm a data breach can cause to your organization's reputation and the resulting loss of customer trust. Because of the far-reaching impacts, determining how much a data breach could cost you can be tricky; per record cost estimates range from $0.58[3] to $154.[2] The lower end of cost estimates includes only direct costs while the upper end includes both direct and indirect costs. One final note on estimating cost relates to the efficacy of measuring the true impact. Neither model referenced for estimating cost applies to data breaches of over 100,000 records. The total cost of a catastrophic data breach is almost impossible to estimate. Unfortunately, most data breaches that have made the news in recent years have been catastrophic as illustrated in Fig. 1.1.

The lag time between compromise and discovery compounds damages incurred from a data breach. Although attackers are able to overwhelmingly compromise an organization and extract data "within minutes,"[3] it can take days for an organization to discover

[1] Enterprise Incident Response Market Booms to $14bn as Attacks and Threats Multiply, ABI Research, Online, https://www.abiresearch.com/press/enterprise-incident-response-market-booms-to-14bn-/.

[2] 2015 Cost of Data Breach Study: Global Analysis, Ponemon Institute LLC, May 2015, downloadable at https://www-01.ibm.com/marketing/iwm/dre/signup?source=ibm-WW_Security_Services&S_PKG=ov34982&S_TACT=000000NJ&S_OFF_CD=10000253&ce=ISM0484&ct=SWG&cmp=IBMSocial&cm=h&cr=Security&ccy=US&cm_mc_uid=94450766918914542954680&cm_mc_sid_50200000=1454295468.

[3] Verizon Data Breach Investigations Report, Verizon, online, http://www.verizonenterprise.com/DBIR/.

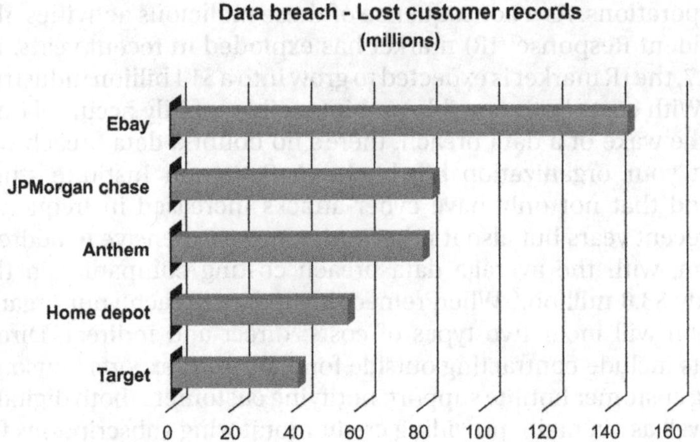

Fig. 1.1 Data breach—lost customer records.

a data breach. In some cases, weeks or months pass before organizations uncover data breaches. In a few extreme examples, data breaches had occurred years before organizational discovery. Following threat forecasting practices will better position your organization to prevent data breaches, and, in addition, when a data breach does occur, threat forecasting practices will enable you to detect the intrusion quickly. But the scope of threat forecasting looks beyond the speed of organizational discovery to the speed of information sharing. It is estimated that "75% of attacks spread from Victim 0 to Victim 1 within one day (24 h)."[3] Sharing knowledge elements, such as indicators of compromise and indicators of interest quickly with applicable platforms, tools and industry groups, can provide real help to likely subsequent victims.

Barriers to Adopting Threat Forecasting Practices

Given the prevalence and cost of data breaches, the need for threat forecasting is obvious. However, many organizations have been reluctant to adopt threat forecasting practices, fearing the costs associated with the required changes. The good news is that threat forecasting relies on a foundation of solid security practices and infrastructure. You may be surprised to discover that your organization has already deployed tools that can be leveraged to begin incorporating a practice of threat forecasting. Moreover, the organizational implementation of threat forecasting practices lends itself to a phased approach, so changes can be made (and any associated costs incurred) incrementally.

Going Beyond Historical Threat Reporting

As previously mentioned, there is no shortage of historical threat reporting. Many prominent companies including Verizon, HP, IBM, Symantec and McAfee release periodic threat reports. These reports detail trends and changes to the threat landscape over the preceding year, quarter or other specified time period. Although reports are generally jam-packed with useful information, the findings can be perceived as out of date since these reports are typically released sometimes months after the time period they cover. Based on these reports, many organizations will make adjustments to their security policies and procedures by focusing on key areas in the reports they have reviewed as applicable to their infrastructure. Because these reports draw data from the past, they are helpful for understanding yesterday's threat landscape. When looking for guidance on the threat landscape of today and tomorrow, these reports have limited use. When reviewing the information provided in these reports it is helpful to be mindful of their key limitations: timing and generalization.

STRENGTHS OF HISTORICAL THREAT REPORTS

Please don't think we're discounting the usefulness of historical threat reports; they are vital tools for any IT organization or security professional. Because our focus is moving toward a threat forecasting mindset, we've spent time in this chapter establishing a need to look beyond historical threat reports. But make no mistake, historical threat reports often present a wealth of information in an organized and concise manner. They are invaluable tools for understanding the security threat landscape and security trends during the period of time in which they cover.

For more information on the uses of Historical Threat Reports, please refer to Chapter 9.

Timing

Threat forecasting goes beyond historical threat reporting. By accounting for the changing threat landscape in real time, risk is reduced, security attacks can be prevented and infrastructure compromises can be detected earlier. Historical threat reporting on the other hand presents the following three challenges for organizations attempting to react to today's landscape. They are stale data, nimble adversaries and emerging technology.

- *Stale data*—As noted, by the time historical threat reports are released the data is often stale. Instead of relying on yesterday's data, threat forecasting aims to quickly analyze data in as close to real time as possible. By analyzing data and trends earlier, you reduce your exposure to risk.
- *Nimble adversaries*—Security professionals aren't the only ones reading historical threat reports. Most adversaries will change their tactics, techniques and procedures once they have been identified. While this aspect of timing is intimately related to stale data, it still bears mentioning.
- *Emerging technology*—Historical threat reports cannot adequately account for emerging technology. By comparison, threat forecasting can account for products on the cutting edge of technology. Shifts in the threat landscape are often indicative of new and emerging technologies in the realms of software, web applications or hardware; threat forecasting can make accommodations for these shifts as they occur instead of falling behind the pace of innovation.

Generalization

Nothing is a substitute for analyzing your own data and combining this with the power of global threat intelligence. Security topics commonly covered in historical threat reports are often subject to a great variation and may change from year to year (or whatever the defined cycle is for the authors of the historical threat report). By employing threat forecasting techniques, your organization can move beyond the generalizations found in historical threat reports to define specific threat profiles facing not just your industry but also your organization.

The State of Regulatory Compliance

In spite of the threats posed by cyber-attacks and data breaches, there are few federal cyber security regulations in place. Most regulations that exist are industry or government specific (at the state or federal level). Today's regulations mostly avoid prescribing specific cyber security measures that should be deployed but instead set forth a standard of a "reasonable" level of security. As such it is best to consider regulatory standards as minimum requirements and build up your security infrastructure accordingly. The following discussion of cyber security regulations is not exhaustive, however is, instead, an overview of selected items we feel currently have the most impact on today's security landscape, standards and best practices. Please thoroughly familiarize yourself with the federal, state and industry-specific regulations impacting your organization.

Industry Specific Guidelines

Although there are relatively few federal cyber security regulations, both the healthcare and the financial sectors are notable because of the established regulations in these industries. If your organization falls into either of these sectors they will be subject to the specified regulatory requirements. Please note that both healthcare and finance are considered critical infrastructures and as such will rely heavily on the National Institute of Standards and Technology (NIST) framework discussed in the next section.

Healthcare Institutions

The healthcare industry and its associated institutions are primarily regulated by the guidelines defined in the Health Insurance Portability and Accountability Act (HIPAA) that was passed in 1996. Prior to HIPAA being enacted, there was basically no generally accepted security standard nor was there any general requirements for the protection of health information. It is comprised of multiple sections, or rules, that must be followed in order to remain in compliance. The rule that we would like to discuss is the Security Rule, as it provides the governance with respect to technology and the protection of electronic protected health information (e-PHI). According to the HIPAA Security Rule Summary,[4] the Security Rule requires covered entities to maintain reasonable and appropriate administrative, technical, and physical safeguards for protecting e-PHI. Specifically, covered entities must:

- ensure the confidentiality, integrity, and availability of all e-PHI created, received, maintained or transmitted
- identify and protect against reasonably anticipated threats to the security or integrity of protected information
- protect against reasonably anticipated, impermissible uses or disclosures of e-PHI
- ensure compliance to the HIPAA Security Rule of all employees.

[4]Summary of the HIPAA Security Rule, Office for Civil Rights Headquarters—U.S. Department of Health & Human Services, Online, http://www.hhs.gov/hipaa/for-professionals/security/laws-regulations/index.html.

The Security Rule defines "confidentiality" as meaning that e-PHI is not to be made available or disclosed to anyone unauthorized to access it and it follows the definition of "confidentiality" as outlined in the HIPAA Privacy Rule. The Security Rule also defines several other key areas that must be considered while operating within the healthcare industry including:

- *Risk Analysis and Management*—Performing regular risk analysis as part of the defined security management process
- *Administrative Safeguards*—Designating an official security officer, putting in place the proper security management process to oversee items like risk analysis and performing regular workforce training
- *Physical Safeguards*—Securing facility access as well as access to workstations and devices that may have access to e-PHI
- *Technical Safeguards*—Having proper access control, auditability, integrity controls and secure transmissions when accessing e-PHI
- *Policies and Procedures and Documentation Requirement*—Adopting reasonable and appropriate policies to comply with all requirements of the Security Rule as well as maintaining a defined document retention policy.

To dive more deeply into HIPAA, please refer to the Health Information Privacy section of the U.S. Department of Health & Human Services website (http://www.hhs.gov/hipaa).

Financial Institutions

The financial industry is subject to a number of different regulatory requirements. A patchwork quilt of regulation exists because the regulatory environment has evolved over several decades. This patchwork nature of legislation can make navigating the regulatory environment challenging for financial institutions. New legislation often not only sets forth added regulatory requirements, but also amends and updates previous legislation and regulatory requirements. The Center for Strategic and International Studies has released a report that covers the evolution of the financial industry regulatory environment in depth; we recommend this report for those interested in a more detailed picture than the one provided in this chapter. [5]

[5] The Evolution of Cybersecurity Requirements for the U.S. Financial Industry, D. Zheng, Center for Strategic & International Studies, Online, http://csis.org/publication/evolution-cybersecurity-requirements-us-financial-industry.

Most of the regulations we will reference in this chapter do not explicitly spell out cyber security requirements. Instead these regulations require organizations to implement "information security systems" for various purposes (e.g., consumer data protection, identity theft protection and reporting requirements). As legislation has been updated and amended over the years, the meaning of "information security systems" has evolved in an attempt to address the needs of today's cyber security environment. Table 1.1 below provides a summary of some legislation pertinent to our discussion; it is not meant to be an exhaustive list.

Table 1.1 Sample Financial Regulations Overview

Legislation	Description
Bank Secrecy Act of 1970 (BSA)	The BSA was designed to combat money laundering, terrorist financing and tax evasion. The BSA implements reporting requirements and processes for defined "suspicious activity." As technology has advanced, new categories of suspicious activity have been added (i.e., electronic intrusion and account takeover.). Advancing technology has also facilitated more efficient reporting processes
Federal Deposit Insurance Corporation Improvement Act of 1991 (FDICIA)	The FDICIA was passed at the height of the Savings and Loans Crisis. As it relates to our discussion, the FDICIA focused on operational assurance and transaction monitoring, requiring organizations to implement information security systems
Gramm-Leach Bliley Act of 1999 (GLBA)	The GLBA was perhaps the first legislation to address concerns emerging in the Internet age. The GLBA introduced security requirements designed to protect consumers' personal data. It also mandated a written information security plan. Additionally, the GLBA requires annual information security training for employees. In 2001, the Federal Trade Commission issued guidelines for GLBA implementation and included specific computer security measures such as using multiple layers of access control, implementing controls to prevent and detect malicious code and monitoring network activity to identify policy violations and suspicious behavior
Fair and Accurate Credit Transactions Act of 2003 (FACTA)	FACTA was a response to the widespread problem of identity theft and focused on information security standards to prevent and combat identity theft

In part because of the lack of specificity in many regulations, financial institutions often turn to the guidance, standards and frameworks provided by outside organizations. Regulatory authorities have found that 90% of financial institutions examined used one or more of these frameworks or standards.[6] We will discuss two of these (PCI DSS and NIST) in the next section, Best Practices, Standards and Framework.

Cyber Security Information Sharing Legislation: Watch this Space

Of course, as the cyber security landscape continues to change, so too will the regulatory landscape. For example, the Cybersecurity Information Sharing Act (CISA) is a bill newly enacted at the time of this writing. The CISA seeks to facilitate information sharing between the government and private companies: "In essence, the law allows companies to directly share information with the Department of Defense (DoD) (including the National Security Agency (NSA)) without fear of being sued."[7] Time is needed before the impact of information sharing legislation can be assessed, but individuals within the information technology and information security community should keep abreast of this and other legislative efforts as they emerge.

Best Practices, Standards, and Frameworks

Because the regulations that do exist mostly avoid prescribing specific cyber security measures, organizations have turned to security standards and frameworks. These provide templates upon which organizations can model their cyber security programs. These standards and frameworks help an organization build a solid foundation of cyber security practices. Following these guidelines will help an organization meet the "reasonable" standard set forth in the few existing federal guidelines. However, to effectively engage in threat forecasting, we believe organizations treat these guidelines as just that. They provide guidance, but you often must add to your cyber security infrastructure and practices in order to reap the benefits of threat forecasting.

[6] Report on Cybersecurity Practices, Financial Industry Regulatory Authority, Online, https://www.finra.org/sites/default/files/p602363 Report on Cybersecurity Practices_0.pdf.

[7] The controversial 'surveillance' act Obama just signed, CNBC, LLC, Online, http://www.cnbc.com/2015/12/22/the-controversial-surveillance-act-obama-just-signed.html.

PCI DSS

First published in May 2009, the Payment Card Industry Data Security Standards (PCI DSS) establishes guidelines for "all merchants and organizations that store, process or transmit" [8] payment card data. Because of the prevalent use of payment cards, these standards reach industries far beyond the financial sector. Although not mandated by federal regulations, compliance with PCI DSS is nonetheless important. Mandatory compliance is established and enforced by major payment card brands. The PCI DSS establishes data security standards for merchants and card processors (see Table 1.2) and outlines an ongoing process of PCI DSS compliance.

If an organization accepts or processes payment cards, it must comply with PCI DSS. The PCI security standards establish reasonable goals for organizations dealing with payment cards and actions required to meet those goals. These goals and requirements are set forth as common sense steps an organization must

Table 1.2 PCI DSS Requirements

Goal	PCI DSS Requirements
Build and maintain a secure network	1. Install and maintain a firewall configuration to protect cardholder data 2. Do not use vendor-supplied defaults for system passwords and other security parameters
Protect cardholder data	3. Protect stored data 4. Encrypt transmission of cardholder data across open, public networks
Maintain a vulnerability management program	5. Use and regularly update anti-virus software 6. Develop and maintain secure systems and applications
Implement strong access control measures	7. Restrict access to cardholder data by business need-to-know 8. Assign a unique ID to each person with computer access 9. Restrict physical access to cardholder data
Regularly monitor and test networks	10. Track and monitor all access to network resources and cardholder data 11. Regularly test security systems and processes
Maintain an information security policy	12. Maintain a policy that addresses information security

[8]Document Library, PCI Security Standards Council, Online, https://www.pcisecuritystandards.org/document_library.

take in order to establish a reasonable level of security. As previously noted, these requirements are a starting point and should be viewed as necessary but not sufficient in organizations striving to build a robust security environment. Table 1.2 summarizes the established goals and requirements.

In order to maintain PCI DSS compliance, the Standards require an ongoing three step process and provide Independent Qualified Security Assessors to monitor and validate compliance. Although the PCI DSS sets overarching industry standards, each major payment card brand maintains its own compliance program. The three step process established by the PCI DSS is in line with cyber security best practices and requires organizations to take steps to assess, remediate and report on their card processing cyber security environments on an ongoing basis (Fig. 1.2). Affected organizations must *assess* their payment card transaction environments, examining cyber security infrastructure, policies and procedure for vulnerabilities. As identified, steps must be taken to *remediate* vulnerabilities. Necessary *reports* must then be compiled to document vulnerabilities identified and steps taken to remediate. As noted, these steps are ongoing, and organizations are expected to incorporate these three steps into their cyber security and IT practices regularly.

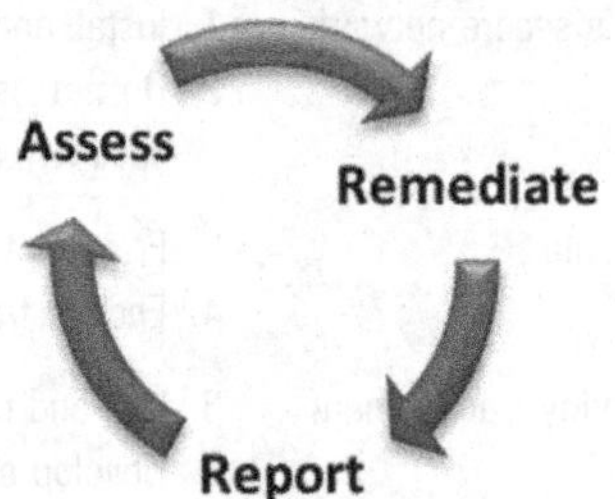

Fig. 1.2 PCI DSS three step process.

NIST Cyber Security Framework

The National Institute of Standards and Technology (NIST) Cybersecurity Framework (CSF) was created specifically to strengthen protection for companies classified as critical infrastructure, however the CSF's sphere of influence has quickly expanded. Organizations beyond those classified as critical infrastructure have also been looking to the CSF for guidance. Although compliance with the CSF standards is voluntary, it has emerged as the standard against which organizations are judged after a data breach occurs.

The CSF is organized into five core functions: Identify, Protect, Detect, Respond, and Recover. These core functions are then further branched into several tiers "which describe the level of sophistication and rigor an organization employs in applying its cyber security practices."[9] Much has been written about the CSF, its core functions and organizational impacts, so we won't dive too deeply into the framework. Please familiarize yourself with these standards as they apply to your organization. When you begin the process of implementing threat forecasting practices in your organization (explained in Chapter 9), the NIST CSF may be a useful starting point when implementing phase one and evaluating your organization's current cyber security practices, policies and procedures.

Defense in Depth

We strongly believe that defense in depth is the correct deployment strategy for any organization. While it may be more convenient to have a single appliance solution from a deployment standpoint, no single appliance is capable of successfully facing all security challenges. Furthermore, we recommend a blended security vendor environment within your infrastructure. Deploying a single vendor environment, even if it is multiple products from that security vendor, only allows you to benefit from one research team. Deploying a blended vendor environment gives you access to multiple research teams who may have access to different attack vectors (i.e., different research data) and thus provides better security coverage. In our book *Blackhatonomics*,[10] we discuss defense in depth in terms of tier 1 and tier 2 technologies. Especially in large corporations, these are the basic building blocks, in the form of tools and technologies, for building a security infrastructure.

Tier 1 Security Technologies

According to current best practices and regulations, the following tier 1 technologies are considered "need to have" when building out a reasonably secure infrastructure:

- Firewall or next-generation firewall
- Desktop anti-virus

[9]Understanding NIST's Cybersecurity Framework, C. Thomas, Tenable Network Security, https://www.tenable.com/blog/understanding-nist-s-cybersecurity-framework.

[10]Blackhatonomics, Chapter 7, W. Gragido, Syngress, 05 December 2012, http://store.elsevier.com/product.jsp?isbn=9781597497404.

- Secure web gateway
- Messaging security
- Intrusion detection/prevention systems
- Encryption (in transit or at rest)
- Security information event management.

Tier 2 Security Technologies

Tier 2 security technologies are often considered "nice to have" when building out a security infrastructure. These technologies are used by organizations with more sophisticated security infrastructures. They are also often purchased by organizations in the aftermath of a major security data breach. Building an infrastructure that combines tier 1 and tier 2 security technologies provides the most robust risk protection. Tier 2 technologies include:

- Advanced threat detection
- Network and desktop forensics
- Network and desktop data leakage protection
- Behavioral-based analysis
- Security/threat intelligence feeds
- Threat forecasting and modeling.

Update and Evaluate Security Products and Technologies

Do not focus myopically on new security vulnerabilities. IT and security teams can display very reactionary behavior when it comes to new vulnerabilities and it is our opinion that you should understand your infrastructure and its potential weaknesses as opposed to reacting to every new announcement (though note we are not saying it is not important to stay abreast of new threats). The Verizon 2015 Data Breach Investigations Report (DBIR) found that when attacks exploit a known vulnerability, "99.9% of the exploited vulnerabilities had been compromised more than a year after the associated common vulnerabilities and exposures (CVE) was published."[3] This highlights the need for organizations to develop thoughtful policies and procedures for installing patches and updates on existing infrastructure (both endpoints and network devices). Organizations that do not keep abreast of release notes and update devices accordingly are at greater risk of a data breach.

Cyber Security and the Human Factor

No discussion of security best practices can be considered complete without factoring in employee behavior. From phishing scams to social engineering, your employees are likely your largest security vulnerability. We believe every employee should be security-minded. Although turning your employees from security liabilities to champions requires organizational effort, a thorough (and engaging) training effort can pay dividends. The Target data breach is believed to be associated with the successful social engineering of one of Target's suppliers. For more information on this data breach, please refer to Chapter 9 (Connecting the Dots).

Today's Information Assurance Needs

Increasingly, organizations are managing information systems and information-related risks with the same thoughtfulness applied to more traditional systems (i.e., computer systems and networks). This practice is known as information assurance (IA). IA experts "seek to protect and defend information and information systems by ensuring confidentiality, integrity, authentication, availability, and nonrepudiation." Essentially, "IA is the process of ensuring that authorized users have access to authorized information at the authorized time."[11] Meeting IA needs today requires the ability to mesh regulatory requirements, best practices and infrastructure needs with a view towards the security landscape of today and tomorrow. By deploying threat forecasting techniques within your organization, you will undoubtedly enhance the security position of your organization. Because the last thing you want to do is invoke your IR plan, threat forecasting helps you head off the next threat.

Welcome to threat forecasting.

[11] Iowa State University Information Assurance Center, http://www.iac.iastate.edu/.

Cyber Security and the Human Factor

No discussion of security best practices can be considered complete without factoring in employee behavior. From phishing scams to social engineering, your employees are likely your largest security vulnerability. We believe every employee should be security minded. Although turning your employees from security liabilities to champions requires organizational effort, a thorough (and engaging) training effort can pay dividends. The large data breach is believed to be associated with the successful social engineering of one of Target's suppliers. For more information on this data breach, please refer to Chapter 2 (Connecting the Dots).

Today's Information Assurance Needs

Increasingly, organizations are managing information systems and information-related risks with the same thoroughness applied to more traditional systems (i.e. computer systems and networks). This practice is known as information assurance (IA). IA experts "seek to protect and defend information and information systems by ensuring confidentiality, integrity, authentication, availability, and nonrepudiation." Essentially, IA is the process of ensuring that authorized users have access to authorized information at the authorized time.[13] Meeting IA needs today requires the ability to meet regulatory requirements, best practices and infrastructure needs with a view toward the security landscape of today and tomorrow. By deploying threat forecasting techniques within your organization, you will undoubtedly enhance the security posture of your organization. Because the last thing you want to do is increase your IA plan, threat forecasting helps you head off the next threats.

Welcome to threat forecasting.

[13] [illegible] University Information Services [illegible]. [illegible]

2

THREAT FORECASTING

Synopsis

In this chapter you will learn about the high-level concepts that are associated with big data collection and how they are applied to threat forecasting. You will learn how the similarities of weather forecasting, epidemiology, and high frequency trading algorithms play an important role in threat forecasting. You will be introduced to concepts that play a greater role in Chapter 3 and beyond, all of which influence the process of forecasting and predicting threat.

Introduction

This chapter will cover the definition of threat forecasting. Additionally, the chapter will cover the reasons why threat forecasting is needed and how this will aid any enterprise and small-to-medium business with information that is specific to industry vertical, geographical location, gold corporate image and bring your own device (BYOD) strategy. Additionally, this will aid in reducing capital expenditure and operating expenditure, which will be explained in great detail within this chapter, as will threat forecasting at a glance and the various modeling technics that frame the components necessary for threat forecasting. Some of the ideas might seem radical but the methods illustrate collectively how we need to look at solving the problem differently and prescriptively in order to reduce organizational risk.

Threat Forecasting

The ability to forecast has been around for thousands of years. Various forecasting models can be applied to financial markets, warfare, epidemiology and meteorology, to name a few. These

Threat Forecasting. http://dx.doi.org/10.1016/B978-0-12-800006-9.00002-1

models study historic and current behaviors and trends with the ability to apply those results to various models in order provide predictable future outcomes. In some of the aforementioned models one could argue that it is more of an art form or that it depends on luck instead of being a science with 100% accuracy. However, the current security controls offered in the market today are becoming smarter and utilizing behavior analytics and mathematics in order to detect and prevent threats. This is a major step forward in solving the time-to-detection problem and insider threat but it is still a reactionary response if the threat is able to make its way to the end-point. Security products are cookie cutters in terms of industry verticals, such as retail, healthcare, banking, manufacturing and government, to name a few. It is akin to throwing an extremely large pored fishing net in the ocean in the hope that you will catch as many fish as possible. Unfortunately, whilst this is great for catching big fish, it does not address the little ones that can escape through the holes. Threat forecasting is tailored to your industry vertical in closing the gap on time-to-detection with a predictable and tailored risk-based model.

The ability to predict behavior and specific outcomes does require precursory knowledge and real-time data. The threat landscape and surface within any organization is highly volatile because we rely on the Internet as a utility. This is largely predicated on the widespread use of smart phones, tablets, laptops, and the Internet of Things. These technologies make up the threat surface, which expands beyond the boundaries/perimeter of any organization regardless of if you are a small-to-medium business or a large enterprise. Additionally, the threat landscape, which consists of malware, vulnerabilities and social engineering, provides the adversary with multiple entry points to gain access and control of your most sensitive data. Since we are reliant on the Internet for work and play, just about everyone is connected 24 h a day, which provides the adversary with plenty of time to achieve their goals in accessing your data. There is a lot of hype around smartphones and tablets as an entry point to a corporate infrastructure, but the truth of the matter is that the adversary is going to be after low hanging fruit and entry points via smartphones and tablets is not high on the list, although they shouldn't be discounted, the risk is low. In order to keep up with the adversary, you have to start thinking like the adversary and augmenting your current security approach, which includes a risk-based approach that fits your industry's vertical and organizational needs. Although there are plenty of security vendors and products to choose from, the truth of the matter is that they are only going to make visible the attacks that they have prior knowledge of in order to detect. Additionally, with the recent security technology pivots designed to cover malware more extensively by utilizing virtualization within a sandbox, they don't truly provide you with the coverage necessary to catch all of the attacks. For example, the Angler exploit kit can tell if a researcher is attempting to execute its code in VMware, VirtualBox, Parallels or other virtual machines as well as a web debugging proxy called Fiddler, which is popular among security researchers. These mechanisms make analysis of Angler a headache for researchers. The ability to augment current security countermeasures with threat forecasting data is going to be necessary if you want to close the current detection gaps in your current security products.

This is an important point because most of the security vendors will release mid-year and yearly trend reports that look back at the most critical vulnerabilities and malware that were prevalent over said period of time. Although this information is interesting and provides a nice read, how are they using this information to better assess the future? The reports are informative about all the threats that you were likely to have been exposed to over the past year, but it honestly does nothing for your security position today and you are likely making buying decisions to protect your infrastructure from threats that have already expired. The graph in Fig. 2.1 illustrates the point that some exploit kits have a short shelf life.

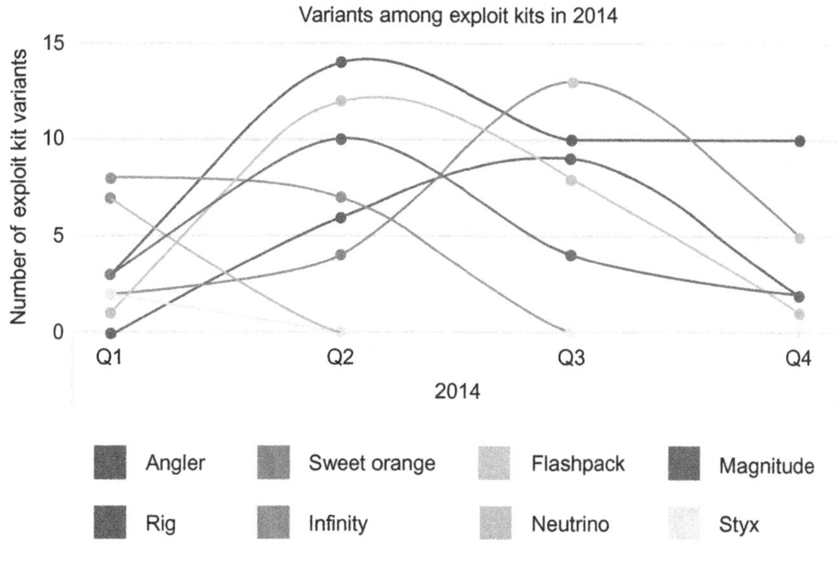

Fig. 2.1 Exploit kit variants timeline.

What is interesting about Fig. 2.1 is that it demonstrates that the Angler exploit kit remained flat in Q3 and Q4, while all the other exploit kit variants started to decline. If you fast-forward to Q2 2015, the Angler exploit kit has branched to several more variants and is still active in terms of exploiting many organizations. Again, historical trend analysis is good, but it really doesn't help anyone to be proactive in terms of being aware of an imminent watch for an attack followed by an imminent warning. These terms (watch and warning) are very similar to what we receive from the national weather service in the event of a tornado. The stance an individual is going to take with a tornado watch is very different from the stance an individual will take with a tornado warning. Additionally, if you are in the path of a tornado, you will take the proper steps to ensure your family is protected. A lot of the same steps can be applied to your corporate security posture. The warning of new and emerging vulnerabilities and malware provides considerable value by keeping you informed with the hope your security vendor has provided you with the proper detection capabilities in being able to stop that new vulnerability or malware. Most organizations will apply the security content/signature updates as standard operating procedure to reduce the risk or patch said systems that are vulnerable. Announcing a new vulnerability or malware would be considered a "watch," but it doesn't really do anything to improve your security position unless your infrastructure is susceptible to the threat (Fig. 2.2).

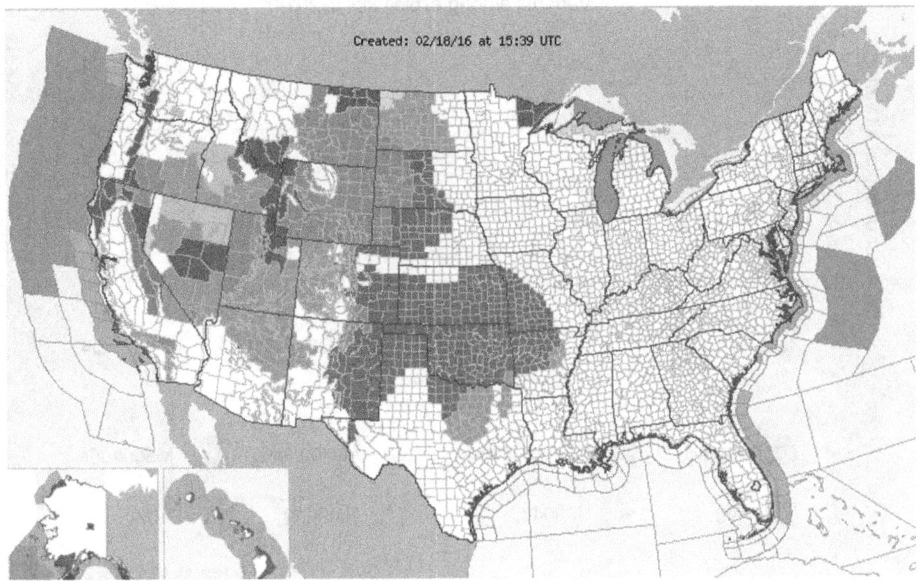

Fig. 2.2 Severe weather alert for tornado warning.

If said vulnerability or malware was targeted specifically at the financial industry and your corporation was a bank and the reports of the said vulnerability or malware were in your current geographical location, you would probably place your organization on high alert. This would require you to have all the pertinent information regarding the exploit and the ability to leverage threat intelligence feeds from other vendors that will help fill the detection gaps of other security vendors. However, the operationalizing of threat intelligence into your process flow is not an easy task and can run into millions of USD for procuring multiple feeds. Threat forecasting is very similar to threat intelligence but goes above and beyond just blanket data. Threat forecasting is differentiated as the data are tailored to your environment with predictable information. Information consolidation and high fidelity data are far more valuable than a cluster of data that may or may not be applicable to your organization. If you are paying for threat feeds and never get a positive event from that data, you have to ask yourself if you are flushing money down the drain that could be used in other areas within your infrastructure. Attacks are becoming more targeted and, therefore, so should the information you are receiving as an augmentation to your current set of security controls that cover the known threats. This is an important point because the authors are not advocating that current security controls are not doing their job, as they are an important aspect of good security hygiene. As we move into 2016 and beyond, the technology sprawl has and continues to exacerbate the risk to all organizations.

Dangers of Technology Sprawl

We have evolved into a highly mobile workforce and society. Many have predicated this on the BYOD movement, but this situation is really driven by accessibility and convenience. The trade-off for accessibility and convenience is risk, as you lose certain aspects of control over assets and staff. This has also been disruptive to most organizations in trying to maintain corporate gold images that are based on user's assets. This is important, as the gold image is approved and typically free of known vulnerabilities, as they are on a regular patch management cadence. One could argue that mobile device management helps fill the gap of being able to manage smartphones and tablets; however, it doesn't always take into account all the mobile devices within an organizations network. This has been a massive challenge to the security industry to attempt to provide access, control, segmentation, detection, and prevention of threats that span the traditional threat surface. In general, most organizations build their security defenses against known security best practices such as NIST, SANS top 20, and ISO 27001. However, security best practices do not take into account the rapid expansion of the threat surface and the security landscape and the relevance of threats to their organization. This requires visibility from the core of the infrastructure to the perimeter and beyond to any mobile devices. There have been strides towards providing visibility within any given infrastructure based on the various security controls that you can deploy. However, visibility is just as important outside of your organization, as stated within this section on mobile devices, and the ever-expanding remote worker. Threat forecasting can almost be compared to user entity/behavioral analytics, except threat forecasting is infrastructure/vertical entity behavioral analytics and forecasting. Mapping the visibility from "inside out" and "outside in" can provide a level of organizational insight that isn't really available…yet.

High Speed Big Data Collection and Surveillance

High-speed data collection in the right places is key to making sure that you have near real-time visibility into malicious targeted data. Those right places need to be the key point of presence points across the globe. Additionally, the high-speed data collection needs to be protected from surveillance from tier 1 actors (Nation States). Unfortunately, we live in a surveillance society where every activity we do online is monitored. The fortunate aspect of threat forecasting is that it is focusing on direct threats to organizations and not caching any metadata other than data that are pertinent to the threat. This is an important point, because that amount of data can be mined and used by tier 1 actors (Nation States). This is something most people are not comfortable with, but it is important to note and emphasis again that this type of data collection is strictly targeted at threat data. This also brings into mind Internet attribution and most security professionals realize that true attribution is extremely difficult to pin point, but regardless of where the threat originated, threat forecasting is only concerned with the traceability of the origin IP address. Meaning, the attack could have originated from China, but is being masked and tunneled through a ToR (The Onion Router) host in Eastern Europe.

The following chapters will go into more detail regarding the full architecture of threat forecasting. However, this does require the ability to harvest data at near line rate (10–100 Gbps) with the ability to quickly process key performance indicators (KPIs) and discard data that are irrelevant to the collection. This is important as it will help reduce the amount of storage needed, but requires significant compute for advanced correlation and queries to the database. A decade ago, this would have required the architecting of a custom hardware platform and custom database schema or highly optimized Oracle database. Today, consumer off the shelf hardware and an open source or licensed databases other than Oracle and Microsoft SQL server with some slight modifications now remove the significant overhead costs and complexity in truly providing the ability to build this yourself. Again, the ability to collect and store network data at near line rate isn't an issue, as this has been solved by various vendors that provide the ability to perform full packet capture utilizing custom application-specific integrated circuit built on the network interface card. The issue with high-speed data collection is not packet capture, but the ability to process, correlate, discover, discard and write to disk at incredibly high rates of speed. This is paramount for the ability to model various KPIs against current and historical data sets.

Threat Epidemiology

The use of various medical science studies such as epidemiology really intersects with various aspects of studying cyber security threats. This is no different from "code reuse," a term that some software developers use when using previously written routines or sub routines and applying them to their code. The basis of threat forecasting is mixing science, mathematics and technology, and applying certain aspects of epidemiology that can be employed in threat forecasting. As an example, the following is a snippet from the National Institute of Health on epidemiology to provide a better basis for understanding the application and use of epidemiology with threat forecasting.

"Epidemiology is the branch of medical science that investigates all the factors that determine the presence or absence of diseases and disorders. Epidemiological research helps us to understand how many people have a disease or disorder, if those numbers are changing, and how the disorder affects our society and our economy."

"Also, many epidemiological estimates try to determine how the number of people affected by a disorder changes over time. The *definition* of a disorder also tends to change over time, however, making estimates more difficult. Even scientists working in the same field at the same time may not agree on the best way to measure or define a particular disorder.

Key terms to know in this field are:

- *Incidence*: The number of new cases of a disease or disorder in a population over a period of time.
- *Prevalence*: The number of existing cases of a disease in a population at a given time.
- *Cost of illness*: Many reports use expenditures on medical care (i.e., actual money spent) as the cost of illness. Ideally, the cost of illness would also take into account factors that are more difficult to measure, such as work-related costs, educational costs, the cost of support services required by the medical condition, and the amount individuals would pay to avoid health risks.
- *Burden of disease*: The total significance of disease for society, beyond the immediate cost of treatment. It is measured in years of life lost to ill health, or the difference between total life expectancy and disability-adjusted life expectancy (DALY).
- *DALY (Disability-Adjusted Life Year)*: A summary measure of the health of a population. One DALY represents one lost year of healthy life and is used to estimate the gap between the current health of a population and an ideal situation in which everyone in that population would live into old age in full health." (http://www.nidcd.nih.gov/health/statistics/Pages/epidemiology.aspx).

A portion of threat forecasting is similar to epidemiology but the focus is on specific industry verticals down to the individual corporation or business instead of people. The concept is similar in terms of understanding the presence and absence of threats over time to really gain insight into past, present and future trends. However, as with certain diseases, they change over time and some mutate. The same thing happens with cyber threats, they change or mutate over time and the "known" threats are detectable regardless of mutation. For example, there can be hundreds of incidences of exploitation for one area of vulnerability. This makes it easy for detection, but it is often too late. The main point with threat forecasting is making sure that you are prepared before that specific threat arrives at your front door. Threat epidemiology is key to understanding current and past trends that will help facilitate the ability to predict future known and unknown threats that are focused on a specific industry vertical down to said organization. The impact of those threats can be measured using epidemiology in terms of "prevalence" and "cost of illness." We can measure the prevalence of an attack as most security vendors track these client statistics by reporting back on those signatures that have had a positive hit. Additionally, this type of data collection also facilitates the security vendor to write better detection capabilities. However, when those defenses are breached the cost of a successful threat has been known to measure multi-millions of dollars, which is an unfortunate effect of a successful breach. For example, the Target breach, according to an article in the New York Times, was estimated to have cost close to "$148 million dollars," even though they had the best security controls that money can buy.

As mentioned in this chapter, art, science and mathematics will play a large role in identifying threats in the decades to come. However, it is the ability to bring all these attributes (art, science and mathematics) together so they work in unison that matters.

High Frequency Security Algorithms

There are a lot benefits in using the science and mathematics around high frequency trading concepts. Platform and intelligent automation is a really important aspect of threat forecasting and during the inception of threat forecasting, almost 4 years ago, there were many methods of accomplishing high-speed calculations and correlation of complex data sets. Pattern matching, statistical sampling and behavioral analytics, and other methods not mentioned, here certainly provide a fundamental foundation for separating clean traffic from malicious traffic. However, multiple engines (pattern matching, statistical sampling and behavioral analytics) are needed but at the same time they need to be fully integrated as one engine and their needs to be an underlying concept/algorithm that ties everything together. There are many different approaches that one could take in connecting the detection and analytics capabilities together at a high-speed rate. This involves classifying the data being written to disk as a transaction and applying similar technics that are used in high frequency trading. The bases of high frequency trading algorithms are time, quantity and price of a said stock and the ability to buy or sell automatically without and human intervention. According Shobhit Seth (http://www.investopedia.com/articles/active-trading/101014/basics-algorithmic-trading-concepts-and-examples.asp), the following are the benefits of algorithmic trading:

- "Trades executed at the best possible prices
- Instant and accurate trade order placement (thereby high chances of execution at desired levels)
- Trades timed correctly and instantly, to avoid significant price changes
- Reduced transaction costs
- Simultaneous automated checks on multiple market conditions

- Reduced risk of manual errors in placing the trades
- Backtest the algorithm, based on available historical and real-time data
- Reduced possibility of mistakes by human traders based on emotional and psychological factors."

These same benefits can be directly applied to threat data as the benefits of using this concept and applying it to threat forecasting will provide the following benefits:

- Threats are detected correctly and instantly
- Reduced time to detection
- Simultaneous automated checks on multiple KPIs globally
- Regression analysis, based on available historical and real-time data
- Reduced possibility of mistakes by human researchers based on a limited skill-set.

The algorithm that threat forecasting uses is a propriety method called the BLAWS algorithm. It functions in a similar way that high frequency trading algorithms perform today, but it also takes in KPIs, which are discussed in another chapter of this book. The sheer volume of data that is being collected and processed demands the ability to perform these functions in nanoseconds with little to no human interaction. This takes the "shake and bake" principle to new levels because if you are not first, you are last and timely collection, detection and dissemination of information to an overall industry vertical and specifically those organizations need to happen quickly.

Summary

This chapter covered the concept of threat forecasting at a very high level. There are many ways to build a new threat detection mouse trap. The ever-expanding threat surface is making it more difficult and complex to reduce risk. This is not to say that current security products are irrelevant or not needed. Threats are becoming more targeted and sophisticated and the ability to have an advanced warning of an attack that is targeting a specific industry vertical and down to a specific organization is far more valuable in allowing an organization to prepare a proper defense.

However, the ability to provide advanced notification is far more effective than detecting a threat when it hits an internal asset. This requires looking at the problem set differently and prescriptively. Threat forecasting may seem like a radical approach but so are the methods that the adversary is using. They are pushing the limits and are very selective in their targets. Again, threat forecasting isn't concerned with who the actor is or what group they belong to. Other security companies are very good at providing those types of data points. A threat will still remain a threat regardless of the actor. The main goal is to cut the signal to noise ratio in the data that are really relevant to your organization. Operationalizing threat data by utilizing STIX, TAXII, and Open IOC into an organizations workflow will be a challenge for some, but as more security products start adopting open standards and embrace sharing it will make the use of threat forecasting more valuable and complimentary to your current security controls.

3

SECURITY INTELLIGENCE

Synopsis

In this chapter you will learn about the high-level concepts of security intelligence and the definition. Additionally, the chapter will go into great detail on all the various key performance indicators (KPIs) that are associated with security intelligence. Furthermore, the chapter will go into how you build your own security intelligence platform. You will learn about the genesis of security intelligence and the level of effort needed to achieve high-fidelity intelligence. It's important to note that all of the intelligence feeds you can buy are equal and there is a lot of overlap, but, honestly, that is a good thing, as some will have other pressing intelligence over others. In the case of security intelligence, multiple security intelligence feeds are better than one.

Introduction

This chapter will define what security intelligence means and why this component is crucial to threat forecasting. Real-time, corroborated and actionable security intelligence is an important piece of threat forecasting. Additionally, this chapter will go into the vetting process of information that will provide the reader with a better understanding of the complexity of security intelligence gathering in actually building, buying or partnering for security intelligence. The chapter will also touch on KPIs and a scoring system that will rate the actual severity and applicability of the security intelligence. This is key but information without value is just that, information that is useless, and in the security world a false positive will lead an analyst down a path that won't yield anything and, furthermore, it's too late at this point because the threat is already inside your network and the whole purpose of threat forecasting is to provide you with information before it ends

Threat Forecasting. http://dx.doi.org/10.1016/B978-0-12-800006-9.00003-3

up on your door step. Understanding what information is intelligence and what is not, is also just as important. Just because it doesn't have a pretty label or an official tag on a hard copy file doesn't mean that it isn't something of interest, or a piece of intelligence. Most of the time it has just been either classified incorrectly or overlooked. Lastly, the chapter covers key indicator attributes of the online processing of small and large data sets followed by the dissemination of security intelligence in the context of threat forecasting.

Security Intelligence

Security intelligence can mean different things to different people. Security intelligence can be best defined as multiple structured and unstructured data sources that can include, but is not limited to, IP addresses, geo IP location, pattern matching, malicious binaries, malicious compound documents such as: PDF files, Microsoft word documents, etc. Additionally, social media can also provide a wealth of intelligence based on hacktivist campaigns against your organization or a specific individual within said organization. Also, the Internet can be scanning for sensitive corporate documents that have been stolen from your corporation or inadvertently leaked by an employee. For the purpose of this chapter security intelligence will be defined in terms of indirect and directed attacks to your organization. Indirect attacks are typically ones that are initiated by a user of a corporation that ended up clicking on a link or email that compromised his or her endpoint (laptop, tablet or mobile device). The directed attack is using known and unknown malware, vulnerabilities, java-based re-directs, to name a few, but the key is that these are directed towards a specific corporation or an entire industry vertical. The biggest thing with structured data and unstructured data is connecting the dots in near real-time and being able to determine what is clean traffic and what is malicious traffic. This also brings up the fact that some, if not most, of the communications will be encrypted; however, most of the malicious traffic is indeed unencrypted and having the ability correlate known and suspicious IP addresses will be key, although the likelihood of those being 99.9% accurate as to malicious activity would be next to impossible. To mitigate this would require a scoring system for the security intelligence to indicate probability as to the severity and classification of the threat.

Information Vetting

Information vetting is an important process in determining the fidelity of the threat intelligence feeds. This requires gathering security intelligence and mapping it to KPIs and the ability to systematically score the security intelligence in an automated fashion that can determine the severity of an impending threat.

KPIs

IP Addresses: This is also known as IP reputation; which IP addresses are consistently changing. The IP addresses are associated with known bad IP addresses for the transport of attacks, command and control and hostile domain name server (DNS) addresses that can redirect a user to a known bad site regardless of if it is an IPv4 or IPv6 address.

Unified Research Locator (URL): These are known bad URLs for the purpose of spreading malware. Although this approach is good, it can affect a known good website by denying complete access. That is why the ability to get down to the uniform resource identifier (URI) will still provide you access to said website but in the event you click on a link within that website it will be able to block that specific malicious unified resource identifier.

GeoIP: This determines and provides the geographic areas where the attack is originating (source) and the destination of an attack down to the specific country and to the city level. The following figure provides an example of what type of information can be extracted from an IP address (Fig. 3.1):

IP Address	Country Code	Location	Postal Code	Coordinates	ISP	Organization	Domain	Metro Code
8.8.8.8	US	Mountain View, California, United States, North America	94040	37.386, -122.0838	Google	Google		807

Fig. 3.1 GeoIP table

Pattern Matching: Provides string matches against known bad strings. The following is an example of something that provides pattern matching:

```
alert http $HOME_NET any -> $EXTERNAL_NET $HTTP_
    PORTS (msg:"ET MALWARE
180solutions Spyware Keywords Download"; flow: to_server,
    established;
uricontent:"keywords/ kyf"; nocase; content:"partner_id=";
    nocase;
```

This example just provides the ability to determine if the traffic destined for your network is indeed known bad. There are other methods that can be used that go beyond pattern matching. For example the ability to perform machine learning and automatically generate security intelligence into pattern matching content. Additionally, the use of behavioral analytics with the use of netflow and sflow can also provide a wealth of security intelligence that can be used for threat forecasting.

Compound Documents: These are known malicious files that are sent by the adversary in the hope that you will open it with a specific application on your laptop, tablet or mobile device. Additionally, it doesn't necessarily take an application but can also be opened with your web browser. The most common compound document is Adobe's portable document format (PDF). The great thing about known bad files is that they contain unique characters that can be tagged, for example badfile.pdf can be tagged with a MD5 or SHA1 checksum.

MD5: aaf8534120b88423f042b9d19f1c59ab

SHA1: ed0c7ab19d689554b5e112b3c45b68718908de4c

However, PDF files are not the only compound documents, that is, file extensions that contain malicious content such as Microsoft Word (.doc and .docx) Microsoft PowerPoint (ppt, pptx, and pps) and Microsoft Excel (.xls and .xlsx). The following is an extensive list possible extensions that could be deemed malicious:

Programs

.EXE—An executable program file. Most of the applications running on Windows are .exe files.

.PIF—A program information file for MS-DOS programs. While .PIF files aren't supposed to contain executable code, Windows will treat .PIFs the same as .EXE files if they contain executable code.

.APPLICATION—An application installer deployed with Microsoft's ClickOnce technology.

.GADGET—A gadget file for the Windows desktop gadget technology introduced in Windows Vista.

.MSI—A Microsoft installer file. These install other applications on your computer, although applications can also be installed by .exe files.

.MSP—A Windows installer patch file. Used to patch applications deployed with .MSI files.

.COM—The original type of program used by MS-DOS.

.SCR—A Windows screen saver. Windows screen savers can contain executable code.

.HTA—An HTML application. Unlike HTML applications run in browsers, .HTA files are run as trusted applications without sandboxing.

.CPL—A Control Panel file. All of the utilities found in the Windows Control Panel are .CPL files.

.MSC—A Microsoft Management Console file. Applications such as the group policy editor and disk management tool are .MSC files.

.JAR—.JAR files contain executable Java code. If you have the Java runtime installed, .JAR files will be run as programs.

Scripts

.BAT—A batch file. Contains a list of commands that will be run on your computer if you open it. Originally used by MS-DOS.

.CMD—A batch file. Similar to .BAT, but this file extension was introduced in Windows NT.

.VB, .VBS—A VBScript file. Will execute its included VBScript code if you run it.

.VBE—An encrypted VBScript file. Similar to a VBScript file, but it's not easy to tell what the file will actually do if you run it.

.JS—A JavaScript file. .JS files are normally used by webpages and are safe if run in Web browsers. However, Windows will run .JS files outside the browser with no sandboxing.

.JSE—An encrypted JavaScript file.

.WS, .WSF—A Windows Script file.

.WSC, .WSH—Windows Script Component and Windows Script Host control files. Used along with with Windows Script files.

.PS1, .PS1XML, .PS2, .PS2XML, .PSC1, .PSC2—A Windows PowerShell script. Runs PowerShell commands in the order specified in the file.

.MSH, .MSH1, .MSH2, .MSHXML, .MSH1XML, .MSH2XML—A-Monad script file. Monad was later renamed PowerShell.

Shortcuts

.SCF—A Windows Explorer command file. Could pass potentially dangerous commands to Windows Explorer.

.LNK—A link to a program on your computer. A link file could potentially contain command-line attributes that do dangerous things, such as deleting files without asking.

.INF—A text file used by AutoRun. If run, this file could potentially launch dangerous applications it came with or pass dangerous options to programs included with Windows.

Other

.REG—A Windows registry file. .REG files contain a list of registry entries that will be added or removed if you run them.

A malicious .REG file could remove important information from your registry, replace it with junk data, or add malicious data.

Office Macros

.DOC, .XLS, .PPT—Microsoft Word, Excel, and PowerPoint documents. These can contain malicious macro code.
.DOCM, .DOTM, .XLSM, .XLTM, .XLAM, .PPTM, .POTM, .PPAM, . PPSM, .SLDM—New file extensions introduced in Office 2007. The M at the end of the file extension indicates that the document contains Macros. For example, a .DOCX file contains no macros, while a .DOCM file can contain macros (http://www.howtogeek.com/137270/50-file-extensions-that-are-potentially-dangerous-on-windows/.)

Since threat forecasting is a relatively new concept that provides the ability to forecast a threat before it arrives at the front door, you have to ensure that all the threat data are high fidelity. This requires a build, buy and partner analysis. In addition to the build, buy and partner analysis you need to perform a statistical scoring analysis that provides the highest probability of the data to determine what would be considered low risk 0–30%, medium risk 31–79% and high risk 80–100%. These risk levels are tied to the KPIs, but more importantly to corresponding IP addresses of major corporations and small-to-medium businesses to email addresses. This is where you can pinpoint risk starting from a specific geographical location, to a city, an industry vertical, a specific corporation and, finally, an individual. There are currently models that exist for scoring threats, as can be seen in the Scientific World Journal, which published the paper "Using a Prediction Model to Manage Cyber Security Threats." Although this type of modeling is tied to CVSS and the risk associated within an organization based on multiple attributes. However, this following snippet from the paper is something can be augmented and used for threat forecasting.

The abstract of the article really provides the outline for using mathematical modeling to predict the impact of the threat:

> *Cyber-attacks are an important issue faced by all organizations. Securing information systems is critical. Organizations should be able to understand the ecosystem and predict attacks. Predicting attacks quantitatively should be part of risk management. The cost impact due to worms, viruses, or other malicious software is significant. This paper proposes a mathematical model to predict the impact of an attack based on significant factors that influence cyber security. This model also considers the environmental information required. It is generalized and can be customized to the needs of the individual organization.*

The authors then go on to explain the importance of prediction models:

Prediction models can be developed to predict different project outcomes and interim outcomes by using statistical techniques. A process performance model adopts the concepts of probability. This can also be explored further by building simulations. Output can be studied as a range. Depending on the predictions, midcourse corrections can be recommended. The model can be simulated to predict final outcomes based on the corrections suggested. It is thus a proactive model that helps the technical analyst to analyze the data and predict outcomes. Analysts can change the data and perform what-if analyses. They can then record these instances and decide on the best option. The model helps analysts decide which lever to adjust to meet the final project goal.

Vulnerability has a positive influence on CVSS score. As vulnerability increases, CVSS score increases and hence the impact on IT assets is high. The influence of network traffic on CVSS is positive. This means that when network traffic is high, the impact of vulnerabilities is high and CVSS score is high. Thus, CVSS score is impacted positively both by vulnerability and by network traffic:

Predicted CVSS Score $= -0.2893 + 0.07174 \times$ *Number of vulnerabilities on the IT application reported by tools* $+ 0.0025 \times$ *Proposed average input traffic for the application for a week measured in KBPS.*[1]

Again, this is just an approach that outlines the ability to use mathematical analysis to predict a specific outcome. The authors have designed similar approaches by using similarities found high-frequency trading algorithms.

Do It Yourself (DIY) Security Intelligence

Although the idea of threat forecasting is conceptual, it can absolutely be accomplished, but it requires the right architecture (sensor and collection nodes), threat data sources, inspection/detection capabilities, modeling and the ability to process and disseminate the output of the intelligence in a timely manner. For the entrepreneur and current security companies, there are many approaches in terms of building this capability yourself using COTS and open source software, providing the ability to

[1] V. Jaganathan, Using a prediction model to manage cyber security threats, *The Scientific World*, Hindawi Publishing, Sep 2014, http://www.hindawi.com/journals/tswj/2015/703713/.

collect, analyze and provide security intelligence that will facilitate the ability to provide timely forecasting information based on various modeling capabilities. Additionally, it will also require software developers, data scientists, UX and malware engineers and reverse engineers, to name just a few. However, there are two other key directions you can take beyond building out your own security intelligence platform, such as buying from and partnering with various security intelligence companies. The key point to remember is there are a lot of data that can be purchased that place a high emphasis on integrity and fidelity.

Build

The build analysis phase will require you to have a keen understanding of what type of hardware is necessary for building out your inspection and collection sensors. Additionally, you will need an analysis platform that has the ability to pull all the KPIs and key indicator attributes. This also requires the ability to utilize a lot of non-general public licenses (GPL) open source software. Otherwise, you will have to provide any update, that is, any software development must be shared with the open source community. This is crucial as any intellectual property or enhancements with a GPL will be lost and others will be able to benefit from the software development cost for said features and enhancements. The following is a high level list that would be required for you to build out your security intelligence platform:

(1) Collection Sensors: Ideally, you would need to place collection sensors in every major geographical location in the world. This can be achieved by leveraging Amazon, Google Cloud Computing, Microsoft Azure, Akamai or RackSpace to name a few. These collection sensors' method of working is twofold; one in their ability to collect data that are passing through them and also in their ability to mimic operating systems with artificial intelligence that mimics a live user that is visiting known or unknown websites with the sole purpose of getting compromised. This information can be harvested and indexed as known good, to be discarded or malicious, and all indicators of compromise are indexed, stored and distributed to the inspection sensors to allow the detection of an incoming attack based on KPIs or key indicator attributes. Building out your own security intelligence isn't trivial as you need to make the information actionable and this process is covered by the inspection sensors.

(2) Inspection Sensors: The inspection sensors just like the collection sensors need to be collocated with the collection sensors,

as they will contain all the indicators of compromise that are tied to the KPIs that where mentioned in the information vetting section. Again, your inspection sensors are only as good as the current information you are feeding them. However, the information from the inspection sensor is also transmitted to a database server that contains all the analytics needed to perform data modeling that utilizes the ability to perform high-speed deterministic and predictive algorithms that perform the analysis that provides the probability of a directed attack against a specific geographical location, industry vertical and specific corporation. Once all this information is correlated and scored it's disseminated to the various organizations that subscribe to receiving the threat data.

(3) Data Modeling Server: The data modeling server is the most important piece of the architecture as it provides all the correlation and data modeling for the data that are coming in from the collection sensor and the inspection sensor. The intellectual property of the data modeling server is completely reliant on the type of deterministic algorithms and high probability analysis with a proper scoring system that provides high-fidelity information that will be disseminated in a timely fashion to your subscribers.

(4) Dissemination: As the sharing of threat information increases, open standards like STIX, TAXII and OpenIOC, to name a few, ensure that all actionable intelligence can be disseminated. However, with imminent threats the dissemination method can be delivered via mobile app, email and text messaging. Additionally, building out a portal will also be required.

The cost of building out such a solution as outlined in points 1–4 will be millions of dollars and it will take 12–18 months of development with a minimum of 6 months of quality assurance testing. The most important aspect is the collection and indexing of data that will allow for historical trend analysis and the ability to run and model data for historic trends for comparison against real-time collection data to determine if a threat is imminent. The multi-million-dollar price tag for such a solution might seem astronomical, but such solutions can be built on a smaller scale and are currently under development; although this might not be practical for a corporation to build out.

Buy

In the buy analysis phase is the ability to short cut a lot of the software development, software and security intelligence feeds that one would have to purchase and this can provide a massive cost saving. This would still require a substantial investment in a collection network, modeling server, which is really the most crucial piece of the architecture along with a way to disseminate the information that will plug into an organization's operational work flow. There are a lot of options when buying security intelligence, but it is most important to buy those with well-defined APIs, which most of the security intelligence vendors provide. The following is a list of a few companies you can purchase security intelligence from:

(1) CrowdStrike
(2) Webroot
(3) VirusTotal
(4) Reversing Labs
(5) Malcovery
(6) Telus

The list is just an example of several companies that can help build out a solid base of legacy and current security intelligence to get you started. However, there are other solutions that will need to be leveraged like Cuckoo sandbox, which is open source, or GFI sandbox to name a couple.

Partner

In the partner analysis phase you determine a security intelligence company you can go to market with and that will provide you with the pieces of the architecture that you are missing for a nominal fee or percentage. This is very similar to the buy analysis, but this is all about achieving time to market in building out your security intelligence platform that will feed into both your inspection server and data modeling server.

This section provides the reader with an understanding at the highest level of the effort and cost associated with building out security intelligence. Although, the data modeling server isn't collecting the security intelligence, it is at the heart of the threat forecasting system.

Key Indicator Attributes

When performing analysis of large or small amounts of data you will quickly discern what a key indicator is and then continue to find the source of the problem, and, as time goes by, patterns will emerge. These patterns are made up of various attributes that in many cases are unique to the data. Individually these would get overlooked as noise and in many cases discarded as junk. One person's junk can be more often than not another person's treasure.

The values that attributes are often categorized by are the payload associations within a major stream of information. This could be something as simple as a pause being removed in a voiceover IP conversation due to network loss in a packet capture replay, where the person replaying the conversation could lose the meaning or context of various words.

Other patterns in what looks like junk often appear when it is correlated with other datasets based on source, destination, time and application/context. While it could be argued that junk correlated with junk equals garbage in garbage out, the differentiator then becomes a case of just because by itself it may pose as junk, peel back a layer and look a little harder with other datasets and it's no longer junk, but a nugget of gold.

Attribute association in a lot of cases is just a matter of widening your gaze. Almost like looking at one of those 1980s 3D posters, after some time you come to realize "oh look it's a sail boat!" At times when looking at larger sets of data it becomes easier to parse the data without excluding the information that looks like junk, as it helps make the sail boat clearer in many cases.

While it is good to look for patterns in large data sets and many are associated with key indicators, it is also important to search for the not-so-obvious patterns. It's not just the context of the attribute but also the time of when the pattern starts and stops. These types of patterns can give indictors as to time zones, locations and sometimes age. This sounds like a lot to take in, but when you put it all together, behavior also plays into the bigger picture.

Looking at the bigger picture of the pattern you see not only when activity starts, but also when it stops or simply takes a break, and you can then start to correlate this information with other associated datasets that have similar peaks and valleys in activity, yet have the same source and that overlay with the other set. Where you may feel that the aggressor is taking a break or stopping, they are just working on another box. This will be discussed in greater detail in Chapter 6—Data Visualization.

Dissemination of Intelligence

Many models exist around the distribution and sharing of information. Many of these methods include encryption, isolated networks, need to know, along with trickle down operations orchestration. Such models are morphed into hybrid solutions of sharing, while keeping to the old adage of keep it secret, keep it safe.

In the past hybrid models that borrow a little from all models have been most prevalent, with the exception of the isolated network, which is commonly reserved for government. This specific network isolation evolves around many layers of classifications where each level has its own security model and isolation networks.

However you chose to disclose and distribute intelligence it's always good practice to do so in relation to the type of intelligence that it pertains to. An example of such information is that of a breach where the aggressor has not only exfiltrated information from your network, but has established a beach head within. Often sharing information across that network also tips off the malicious actor that you have found information and are making plans to eliminate the threat.

Basing the theory of dissemination around the beach head example, it would be best to create a new CA server offline and generate many certificates for those involved in the breach investigation, including certificates for upper management, until the threat has been eliminated. Distribute the certificates and keys through alternative channels that aren't directly connected to the breached network, this ensures that all communications are encrypted and obfuscated from the malicious actor.

Making sure that all communications are encrypted the investigation can continue to take place from a clean system that isn't the investigator's main workstation. This is so that in the event the investigator becomes a target of the malicious actor, not all information will be exposed, only that which has been discovered during that time frame.

Security posture and enforced security policies will also help mitigate many information leaks while the investigation takes place, allowing you to get closer to the target, who is still at this time unaware that the security organization knows of their existence in the network.

Keeping the information sharing to strictly isolated networks that aren't connected to the primary network, and forcing all security personnel to use multiple workstations, ensures security of the intelligence until such time as the problem arises from within the isolation and the malicious actor becomes a trusted member.

The need to know policy works well in most cases, until the information is shared with member of the team who feels that every member of your security organization has a need to know. This is an event that normally only happens once and, depending on the type of event, ends up being a resume rendering one for the team member who felt that everyone needed to know. Sadly once the news is out, it often spreads like a wild fire and the security team, whilst still investigating the breach, has to start fielding awkward questions as to what happened, how it happened and when it will be remediated. They now need to work overtime as a malicious actor may get notified via loose communications regarding the breach and another issue is that systems administrators may inadvertently taint evidence by changing mac times on files and generally compounding the problem for the investigation team.

Operations orchestration is not as commonly practiced for incident response as it is for notifying larger community groups that handle sensitive or classified information on a regular basis over a largely distributed isolated network. Such an organization's common practice is to send a notification over regular channels regarding a notification on the isolated network and to send confirmation of information and intelligence received, as well as its having been acted upon and, in many cases, implemented.

Twenty-four-hour operations' facilities often see the orchestration model as the automated means to an end as many functions including, but not limited to, incident response can be automated. These tasks are mostly minor issues that crop up from known malware and virus infections to tracking the status of a security event and following it through with a fully documented process and write up of step-by-step procedures at the most mature levels. Unfortunately, not many organizations can claim that level of maturity.

So what is the best way to disseminate information and understand the level of classification for a particular piece of information at which point it is deemed intelligence? Each answer will be different based on the topology and landscape of your ecosystem.

To help you figure out what intelligence looks like it is important to define the weaknesses in your environment and have a good understanding of what each tool does and how it works with the other security tools. Not many organizations have figured out that it's not the number of tools that you have but the placement, capability and augmentation of those tools that, not only make a safe haven for sharing of information, but also help gather and make sense of information.

Further breaking this problem down into an ingestible equation, is to define your required safe haven:

- Encrypt communications
- Compartmentalization
- Protected reporting
- Orchestration of incident response procedures

Safe communications are a must have in any organization. Along with making discussions about security issues and sharing of information easier (beware of the caveats with encryption) comes the risks of unwanted covert channels and poor key escrow management.

Compartmentalization of security teams. Not to say that the left hand doesn't need to know what the right hand is doing, but not everyone needs to know every detail of every bug found or breach detected.

Every security incident needs to be documented, while this sounds like it's stating the obvious, to many the question is: "At what level does an incident or event need to be documented?" The answer: "The moment it becomes one." For the simple reason that learning from the past as to how a specific event or incident was handled, may help shape how the next incident or event can be better handled or prevented in the future.

The threat landscape of any organization can be altered for the better by having an understanding of not just what has happened in the past to other similar organizations, it is as important to learn from its own past in order to assess how to prevent potential possible threats and attack vectors in the future.

Orchestration of information/intelligence dissemination to a closed network is key to the success of larger distributed groups that share and exchange threat intelligence, as they are in many cases connected to the same infrastructures or share a common goal.

In a highly public arena where it seems like every major breach is posted on pastebin and zone-h for hacker recognition, a breach is no longer something that you keep behind closed doors until you have figured out what has been lost. It's now public information, and you have to play damage control. The point is that until you know what it is you are dealing with, information can be taken out of context and twisted to suit the person wielding it without any understanding, other than this is evidence of a breach. This may attract many trolls who will try and scour and glean any useful information from the remnants in the logs and copies of files posted.

Summary

Security intelligence is a very broad area and as mentioned earlier can mean different things to different people. Security intelligence was defined as multiple structured and unstructured data sources that can include, but is not limited to, IP addresses, geo IP location, pattern matching, malicious binaries, malicious compound documents such as: PDF files, Microsoft word documents, etc. As the Internet continues to move toward the use of Transport

Layer Security (TLS) and Secured Socket Layer (SSL), the reliance on IP reputation will be an important point for correlating traffic, but the ability to launch artificial intelligent virtual machines that act like a legitimate user will also be needed to verify and validate encrypted traffic. This is important as collecting security intelligence by breaking TLS/SSL and/or VPN encrypted traffic would be a violation of privacy, not to mention regulatory compliance.

The chapter also discussed how information vetting is an important process in determining the fidelity of the threat intelligence feeds and KPIs. Those KPIs are useless without the ability to correlate the security intelligence against high value assets, which are corporations and high-level individuals of said corporation. Additionally, having a scoring system for the fidelity of the security intelligence is a point that needs to be reiterated because this is going to be pivotal in providing the security intelligence that will either provide a threat watch or threat warning message to said target, that is, a corporation or high-level individual in the corporation.

This chapter also covered the entire threat forecasting platform in terms of building out your own security intelligence. The authors felt this was an important diversion that outlines the complexity of building out security intelligence in a build, buy and partner analysis. Some of the authors have already started building out said solutions and based on their experience in building security solutions for some of the largest security companies in the world, it was important to capture that specific journey. Although they choose the build path for various reasons, this type of capability, that is, threat forecasting, is going to be necessary in order to keep up with the ever-changing threat landscape and threat surface. The changing threat surface keeps expanding with the rapid adoption of mobile devices, tablets and Internet of Things (IoT), which should be renamed the Internet of Everything (IoE). The threats against specific applications are going to be more focused on programing languages such as Apple's Xcode and other mobile programming languages that will allow the adversary (state or on-state-sponsored actors) to hook the programming languages that will allow them the ability to exploit the containerization of mobile applications that are typically sandboxed from other applications. However, at some point the adversary needs a way to access said mobile device and the ability to control and exploit other applications and ultimately information. This might sound like a very difficult task but it's easier to go after the source "code" as any programming language that can be hooked, it doesn't matter what application the software developer creates, the backdoor will be in place for the adversary to have total control of and the ability to survey their target. To be clear this is a practice that is in current use by Intelligence and Federal organizations worldwide. The key point to take away is that if state-sponsored actors have this insight, you can guarantee that others are doing so as well. The purpose of this digression is to point out that KPIs span much further than what has been described in this chapter.

Although the idea of threat forecasting was talked about in a conceptual context when the research for this book started almost 3 years ago, it's almost a reality today. To reiterate the point: "it can absolutely be accomplished but requires the right architecture (sensor and collection nodes), threat data sources, inspection/ detection capabilities, modeling and the ability to process and disseminate the output of the intelligence in a timely manner." The build buy, partner for building out security intelligence that will ultimately lead to threat forecasting provides any entrepreneur and current security companies with the ability to do this themself using COTS, open source software and providing the ability to collect, analyze and provide security intelligence that will facilitate the ability to provide timely forecasting information based on various modeling capabilities.

You will quickly discern the key indicators of performance when performing analysis of large or small amounts of data and then continue to find the source of the problem as time goes by and as patterns emerge. These patterns are made up of various attributes that in many cases are unique to the data. Individually these would get overlooked as noise and in many cases be discarded as junk. One person's junk can be, more often than not, another person's treasure. These patterns are important as they tie in to pattern matching, which crosses over to a KPI but contains a lot more information. The emphasis is placed on the values that attributes are often categorized by, which are the payload associations within a major stream of information. This could be something as simple as a pause being removed in a voiceover IP conversation due to network loss in a packet capture replay, where the person replaying the conversation could lose the meaning or context of various words. Again, this is highly valued information that needs to be built in to the security intelligence collections.

Intelligence from the field is also needed for the obvious reasons of not just anticipation of an attack or breach, but to aid and prepare you for such an attack or breach, so that you can put as many counter measures around your critical infrastructure as possible and prevent the instantiation of a beach head from an attacker. Other methodologies are more expensive 24 h security operations solutions with continuous network security monitoring and advanced preventative automated decisions based on a weighted threshold of threat frequency, criticality and event type. This can be automated in many ways to form a tier 1 solution being fed data from tier 2 or at a simpler level of tier 1 as the poverty line becomes harder to overcome with ever shrinking IT and security budgets.

Lastly the dissemination of the security intelligence is important as many models exist around the distribution and sharing of information. Many of these methods include encryption, isolated networks, need to know, and trickle down operations orchestration. Such models are morphed into hybrid solutions of sharing, but keeping to the old adage of keep it secret, keep it safe. In the authors' experience, hybrid models that borrow a little from all models have been most prevalent, with the exception of the isolated network, as that is commonly reserved for government. This specific network isolation evolves around many layers of classifications where each level has its own security model and isolation networks. Nonetheless having an operational flow of data dissemination that is able to snap into any organization will allow said corporation to digest the information and, more importantly, use the information to provide the necessary protection before the threat arrives at their front door.

4

IDENTIFYING KNOWLEDGE ELEMENTS

Synopsis

Being able to manage indicators of attack (IOA), indicators of compromise (IOC), and indicators of interest (IOI) is of paramount importance in today's world. Whether you are working to defend an enterprise from attack, mitigate the risk associated with an intrusion, or just trying to work toward a better way of sharing indicator and indicator object data, the ability to share in some fashion should be taken seriously. In this chapter you will learn about the importance in being able to distinguish between intelligence and information, while being introduced to the concept of increasing the signal-to-noise ratio. You will be guided through the most common frameworks and standards in the industry today for indicator and indicator object sharing and will be introduced to concepts that speak contextually to the threats represented by said indicators. Ultimately you will be introduced to concepts that play a greater role in Chapter 5 and beyond, all of which influence the process of forecasting and predicting threat.

Introduction

The world is a much more complex place than it was a decade ago. The impact and extent of sharing what we commonly call IOC today, was small scale and minimal; most relegated to trust communities set up among information security vendors, industry trust communities, or information sharing analysis centers (ISAC) and computer emergency response teams (CERT). Over time as more and more information became available about the threat landscape, more and more sharing took place. Whether we were sharing information about malicious IP addresses, domains, MD5s or

Threat Forecasting. http://dx.doi.org/10.1016/B978-0-12-800006-9.00004-5

malware samples, the sharing grew but the pieces of information derived and distilled from that sharing—the indicators—were not necessarily shared universally or if they were, they were not easily consumed by the disparate technological platforms ranging from end point agents, to network based security devices, to Security Information Event Management (SIEM). As a result, many people and organizations began recognizing the need to devise ways in which to extract salient information from threat research endeavors, consume them and package them for reuse and consumption by themselves and, eventually, other organizations. Concepts such as IOA were introduced to add more contextual relevance to IOCs and IOI making them more valuable than if they were just stand alone indicators. These indicators worked from the premise that the signal-to-noise ratio had already been met and that participating organizations were taking full advantage of the schemas, standards, and frameworks that were being brought to market and made freely available to those in need. In this chapter we will explore these concepts collective while differentiating their key points. We will demonstrate the merits of each schema, framework, or standard identified, while identifying potentials for failure, which warrant amendment. Individuals and organizations alike will be able to gain key insights into these offerings, which will enable them to make intelligence decisions regarding their employment and use within their environments.

Defining Knowledge Elements

Intelligence Versus Information

As we begin our discussion on knowledge elements within this chapter we thought it would be important to take a moment to explain the difference between intelligence and information. Many people use these terms interchangeably yet they are unique and carry their own distinct meaning. *Intelligence*, as defined by Merriam-Webster is:

- the ability to learn or understand things or to deal with new or difficult situations
- secret information that a government collects about an enemy or possible enemy; also: a government organization that collects such information

Information as defined by Merriam-Webster is:

- knowledge that you get about someone or something: facts or details about a subject
- a service that telephone users can call to find out the telephone number for a specified person or organization

Acknowledged by individuals and organizations alike for their differences they often remain used synonymously. For many the only difference lies in the second proposed definition of the word information, which describes a service, provided by telecommunications services the world over for their clientele. Though their differences are pronounced, understanding the unique relationship that exists between them is paramount to any individual or organization seeking to develop and establish a service that focuses on threat forecasting and predictive analysis. Contrary to popular belief, within certain communities and elements within the information security industry these terms, when use appropriately with authority, are not banal but rather fresh and inspired as they bring together key concepts germane to people, objects, locations, systems, and networks that can and often are used to achieve a wide variety of ends by many different types of actors and defenders.

Therefore, understanding the definitions of the words intelligence and information cannot be stressed enough. Understanding and being able to apply knowledge related to diverse subjects and situations where the focal points may vary from diverse threat actors (ideologically driven, criminal, nation state proxy, or state sponsored) and their tactics, techniques, and procedures (TTPs) to real-world targets (e.g., individuals, businesses/organizations, entire industry verticals, or government/military) from a Target of Interest (ToI)—a target which an attack is planned against after much preparation, and Target of Opportunity (ToO)—a target on which attack is unplanned and which is attacked upon favorable presentation or unexpected discovery or appearance.

A Quick Note About the Signal-to-Noise Ratio Metaphor

Like intelligence and information, two other terms come into play when beginning discussions related to cyber threat intelligence, threat forecasting and predictive analysis. The two terms in question are signal and noise. We often refer to them in terms of "ratios" or the number of times one value contains or is contained within the other value, when in fact what we're really referring to (unless we're engineers) is the metaphor associated with them. As we've noted with respect to the terms intelligence and information, there is a great degree of disparate thought surrounding signal and noise within the industry. However, we would be remiss were we to write not only a chapter but an entire book without introducing, explaining, referencing, and reinforcing these concepts based on our real-world and academic understanding of their use and application.

So what is the signal-to-noise ratio? The signal-to-noise (commonly abbreviated SNR or S/N in scientific circles) is a form of measurement used in certain applied sciences (electrical engineering for example), which compares the level of desired signal or the level of a function that conveys information about the behavior or attributes of some phenomenon.[1] The use of signal in this context often evokes images of data or telecommunications environments, signal processing or electrical engineering. Signal is compared against background noise or unwanted sound; sound that interferes with the overall signal quality making receipt, interpretation, and response to a message or piece of intelligence or information extremely difficult. Over the course of many years this metaphor for signal-to-noise ratio has come to be used quite broadly, especially in those cases where we may be discussing messages (intelligence or information) that need to be received, interpreted, and responded to in as crisp a manner as possible. With regard to this book and specifically this chapter, our goal is to ensure that the signal-to-noise ratio is quite low, so that we may maintain a precise focus on our goal of sending and receiving messages (intelligence and information concepts) germane to the topic of threat forecasting and predictive analysis. Because of the net effect that that the signal-to-noise ratio may have on our work, whether we are electrical engineers triaging a routing or switching platform, or information security oriented individuals focused on cyber threat intelligence as it relates to threat forecasting and predictive analysis, we must strive to achieve the highest levels of fidelity and purity in signal possible.

A Brief Note on IOCs and IOIs

As we make our way through this chapter, two concepts shall be introduced which will be critical to the reader as he or she endeavors to comprehend cyber threat intelligence, threat forecasting and predictive analysis. These two concepts or, perhaps put more appropriately, these two acronyms account for many sub-categories of knowledge and understanding that we will explore. It should also be noted that though in most instances these concepts, specifically the IOC and the IOI, are solely relegated to the world of machine-oriented interpretation systems.

[1] https://books.google.com/books?id=QBT7nP7zTLgC&pg=PA1&hl=en#v=onepage&q&f=false

However, there are many instances and cases where some of these sub-categories will be extremely important on a non-machine-oriented level and thus will have an impact or some material bearing on work being conducted by cyber threat intelligence analysts the world over.

Identifying Something Important Through the Use of IOAs, IOCs, and IOIs

IOAs, IOCs, and IOIs aid us in understanding important things that are occurring within our hosts and networks. Some of these things may be benign yet meaningful from an administrative perspective while others may be indicative of a state of compromise within the environment affecting one or more hosts and the infrastructure itself. In the broad case of threat forecasting and predictive analysis, having a healthy understanding of IOAs and their relations to IOCs and IOIs is of paramount importance.

Through understanding what is critical to a threat actor or adversary (that which is contextually relevant to an exploit and compromise), we can gain key insights into what may occur or may be associated with the modus operandi—particular way through which a threat actor or adversary conducts him- or herself within enterprise environments. As we will see in the following sections, having a solid understanding of IOAs, IOCs, and IOIs will aid us in understanding several factors of the events taking place within our enterprise environments and regarding those who may be responsible for them. This information is critical if your organization believes or has reason to believe that it is a ToI. In the section named Types of Knowledge Elements, we will explore IOAs, IOCs, and IOIs in more detail.

Types of Knowledge Elements

Within the information security and threat intelligence disciplines there are many types of knowledge elements. Some are oriented toward machines and the consumption of knowledge elements by machines, such as firewalls (FW), intrusion detection systems (IDS), intrusion prevention systems (IPS), and endpoint threat detection and response (ETDR) platforms, while other knowledge elements are oriented towards the combination of machines and human analysts. In the following sections we will discuss in detail the two primary categories of knowledge elements associated with information security, threat intelligence, and threat forecasting and predictive analysis.

IOA or Pre-attack Indicators

Defined by CrowdStrike and Intel/McAfee in 2014, the term IOA carries with it a different meaning from its peer terms IOC and IOI. The term IOA is similar in nature to a term commonly used in law enforcement scenarios, the Pre-Attack Indicator.[2] According to Intel/McAfee an IOA is the unique construction of unknown attributes, IOCs, and contextually relevant information (including organizational intelligence and risk) into a dynamic, situational picture that guides response.[3] CrowdStrike defines an IOA differently. According to a blog post written by CrowdStrike on this topic in December of 2014, an IOA can be defined as a series of actions that an adversary must conduct in order to succeed.[4] CrowdStrike uses the example of a spear phishing attack to illustrate their point regarding IOAs. They go on to build out a scenario that looks something like the following:

- Campaign ensues
- Campaign relies on convincing or persuading the target to click on a link or open a document that will infect a machine
- Once successfully compromised, the adversary will execute another process, hide in memory or on disk in order to establish and maintain persistence
- Command and control communications will be established with a C2 sit where in the adversary informs his handlers that he awaits further instructions

According to both Intel/McAfee and CrowdStrike the IOAs will be concerned with and focus upon execution of these steps (in this scenario the steps associated with the spear phishing attack), the intent of the adversary (reasoning/rationale/goal behind the attack and its success) and the outcomes of the efforts put in place. So in the case of the IOA we're concerned with a broader, overarching condition and state that may include, among other things, IOCs, but completion of the mission is not necessarily solely dependent upon these alone. Understanding IOAs is of paramount importance and critical to understanding the mindset and rationale of an adversary. Certainly CrowdStrike and Intel/McAfee do, as do the authors. And so it is in the best interests of the analyst and the organization impacted to understand IOAs as deeply as possible.

[2] https://www.policeone.com/police-products/training/articles/1660205-Pre-attack-indicators-Conscious-recognition-of-telegraphed-cues/

[3] http://www.mcafee.com/us/resources/solution-briefs/sb-indicators-of-attack.pdf

[4] http://www.crowdstrike.com/blog/indicators-attack-vs-indicators-compromise/

Indicators of Compromise

Unlike IOAs, IOCs are forensic artifacts or remnants of an intrusion that can be identified on a host or network.[5] They are not behaviorally driven (in other words they do not necessarily reflect the behavior or intent of a threat actor or adversary) nor are they tied to extensions of TTPs. They are however, rooted in artifacts that can be extracted from hosts within the network or the elements which comprise the network itself leading to the entry point of a threat actor and his or her exfiltration point(s). Common examples of IOCs include:

- IP address
- IPv4
- IPv6
- URL and FQDN+Path
- MD5 hash
- SHA-1 hash
- File Name
- File Type
- Windows Registry Key
- Windows Driver

In many cases identifying IOCs, once an analyst is trained in what to look for, is quite simple and leads to examples such as those provided in Table 4.1.

Table 4.1 Examples and Descriptions of IOCs

Indicator of Compromise (IOC)	Description of the IOC
IPv4	105.103.125.129
IPv6	2002:0:0:0:0:0:105.103.125.129
URL (FQDN+Path)	islam20134.no-ip.biz
MD5	a07c79ed7a30c5408d6fb73b4c177266
SHA-1	992cbd54688030d9afd631946f4698de078638bf
File name	Server.exe
File type	PE32 executable (GUI) Intel 80386 Mono/.Net assembly, for MS Windows

In many instances people have mistakenly associate IOCs with behaviors observed in hosts or within network enterprise

[5]https://blogs.rsa.com/understanding-indicators-of-compromise-ioc-part-i/

environments (conflating the term IOC with IOA). For example, in 2013 the online information security magazine Dark Reading posted an article titled "Top 15 Indicators of Compromise."[6] The article provides examples of what they purport to be "Indicators of Compromise."

However, the list provided by Dark Reading is actually better aligned with the definition we saw above for IOAs or TTPs. In their list they include observable behaviors such as:

- Unusual outbound network traffic
- Anomalies in privileged user activity
- Geographical irregularities
- Other log-in red flags
- Swells in database read volume
- HTML response sizes
- Large number of requests for the same file
- Mismatched port-application traffic
- Suspicious registry or system file changes
- DNS request anomalies
- Unexpected patching of systems
- Mobile device profile changes
- Bundles of data in the wrong places
- Web traffic with unhuman behavior
- Signs of DDoS activity

If we are to assume that our definition of IOCs is true and accurate and that IOCs apply to machine-oriented platforms such as firewalls, IDSs, IPSs, ETDR platforms, and advanced threat detection (ATD) products among other platforms, as well as to information security and cyber threat intelligence analysts respectively, then we must dismiss lists such as these in relation to IOCs and relegate them to behaviors associated with IOAs and TTP. This is important due to the fact that there remains some degree of debate as to what an IOC is (exactly) within the information security industry, how they are used, and to what degree. Not to mention the fact that, at least in the eyes of certain organizations and industry subject matter experts, IOCs are merely attributes of IOAs. In the next section we will explore a concept that is not as well known as that of the IOC, yet still provides a tremendous amount of value to those seeking to understand more about their host and network environments while attempting to forecast and predict threat activity.

[6]http://www.darkreading.com/attacks-breaches/top-15-indicators-of-compromise/d/d-id/1140647

Indicators of Interest

Like IOCs, IOIs may include forensic elements and artifacts associated with the remnants of an intrusion or compromise of a host or networks, however, they typically address information that acts in a supporting role to the identification and definition of an IOC. In many instances, IOIs themselves will contain or provide insight into IOCs lending themselves closer (by definition) to IOAs than IOCs. Examples of IOIs may include:

- HTTP session
- 'WHOIS' information
- DNS Queries
- Autonomous system network number
- User accounts
- Country of operation
- Packet capture

In the following example we will provide information related to an IPv4 address that will demonstrate information that can be used in defining contextually relevant information within or pertaining to an IOI, in this case an IP address associated with known malicious domains (Table 4.2).[7]

Table 4.2 Examples of Indicators of Interest (IOIs)

Indicator of Interest	Data	Detail
IP Address		
	Type-IPv4 Address	105.103.125.129
	WHOIS	% This is the AfriNIC Whois server. % Note: this output has been filtered. % To receive output for a database update, use the "-B" flag. % Information related to "105.96.0.0 - 105.111.255.255" % No abuse contact registered for 105.96.0.0 - 105.111.255.255 inetnum: 105.96.0.0 - 105.111.255.255 netname: TA23-new descr: Telecom Algeria country: DZ org: ORG-TA23-AFRINIC admin-c: DN2-AFRINIC tech-c: SD6-AFRINIC status: ALLOCATED PA mnt-by: AFRINIC-HM-MNT mnt-lower: DJAWEB-MNT mnt-domains: DJAWEB-MNT source: AFRINIC Filtered parent: 105.0.0.0 - 105.255.255.255 organisation: ORG-TA23-AFRINIC org-name: Telecom Algeria org-type: LIR country: DZ address: Complexe Informatique des PTT address: RN 36 Ben Aknoun address: ALGER phone: +213 92 12 24

Continued

[7] https://urlquery.net/report.php?id=1451853193990

Table 4.2 Examples of Indicators of Interest (IOIs)—*Cont'd*

Indicator of Interest	Data	Detail
		fax-no: +213 92 12 08 admin-c: SD6-AFRINIC tech-c: SD6-AFRINIC mnt-ref: AFRINIC-HM-MNT mnt-ref: DJAWEB-MNT mnt-by: AFRINIC-HM-MNT source: AFRINIC Filtered person: DJOUAHRA Naima address: ALGERIE TELECOM INTERNET DJAWEB address: Complexe Informatique des PTT address: Route Nationale N 36 Ben Aknoun address: ALGER—ALGERIA phone: +213 21 92 20 04 fax-no: +213 21 92 20 04 nic-hdl: DN2-AFRINIC mnt-by: AT-MNT source: AFRINIC Filtered person: Security Departement address: Alger phone: +21321911224 fax-no: +21321911208 nic-hdl: SD6-AFRINIC source: AFRINIC Filtered
	DOMAIN	islam20134.no-ip.biz
	User accounts	N/a
	Country of operations	Algeria
	Name/Identity/ Contact Information	DJOUAHRA Naima ALGERIE TELECOM INTERNET DJAWEB address: Complexe Informatique des PTT address: Route Nationale N 36 Ben Aknoun address: ALGER—ALGERIA phone: +213 21 92 20 04 fax-no: +213 21 92 20 04 person: Security Departement address: Alger phone: +21321911224 fax-no: +21321911208 nic-hdl: SD6-AFRINIC source: AFRINIC Filtered

Publicly Defined Knowledge Elements

As we have seen previously in this chapter, knowledge elements take on many forms. In this section we will be describing several of the most popular publicly defined knowledge elements for review and consideration. Before we begin, let's take a moment to review our definition of an IOC. An IOC is a forensic artifact or remnant of an intrusion that can be identified on a host or network. Each of the following publicly defined knowledge elements deals with IOCs in one way or another. NOTE: as at the time of writing there is no universally adopted or ratified standard for IOC sharing. Though there are several options to choose from, there remains a fairly heated debate as to which standard affords the users with the greatest degree of flexibility and usefulness. It is not uncommon to find adherents to one standard or another rather adamant about their choice of element. This is to be expected, as most adherents are end users and consumers of the standards. They will have a vested interest in seeing whichever standard they have chosen successfully adopted, utilized, and supported, not only within their own environments, but also within the industry itself. In this section we will explore four standards options for IOC sharing: OpenIOC, Cyber Observable eXpression (CybOX), Incident Object Description Exchange Format (IODEF) (RFC5070), and IOCBucket.com.

OpenIOC

OpenIOC is a standard that was first pioneered and championed by the team at Mandiant (now FireEye). Since its inception it has become the defacto standard for machine-oriented data point sharing (specifically for data points related to, or determined by, IOC). Mandiant developed the standard because they had recognized both the need for a solution and realties that dictated it:

- *Sophisticated Indicators:* Traditional methods of identifying security breaches no longer worked. Mandiant found that intruders too easily circumvented simple signatures; they recognized the need for a better way. They decided that the best solution for all organizations would be to be able to communicate whether or not there were attackers on their networks and hosts in an efficient, reliable, and fast manner. The solution it seemed lied in the ability of a provider (in this case Mandiant) to deliver such data in a machine-oriented (digestible) format that would see the greatest source of delay—the human delay—removed from the equation and from threat intelligence sharing.
- *Advanced Threat Detection:* Mandiant was able to prove that by using the OpenIOC framework an organization could achieve a state where the most advanced threat-detection capabilities were not only possible, but also available. So confidant were they that they built a community dedicated to the OpenIOC standard (also known as an initiative) through which an organization could benefit significantly from the net effect of threat intelligence organizations within a given industry vertical in addition to those across the Fortune 1000.
- *Extendable and Customizable:* Recognizing early on that any solution that they devised would need to be adaptable and flexible, Mandiant decided only through offering extensions and customization would the standard be accepted broadly beyond their own use cases. As a result, OpenIOC offers organizations the ability to use Mandiant's field tested and proven IOCs while also affording them the ability to create their own custom sets of IOCs.

- *Codification:* The need to be able to codify or arrange in systematic order information brought into an organization for consumption in the form of an IOC was crucial to the success or failure of this standard. Mandiant defined the standard in such a way so that any and all data is easily codified and ready for use.
- *Satisfaction:* Through the development of this standard, Mandiant achieved a sense of satisfaction. They had seen something grow out of their own use cases, be adopted across their user community and then be recognized for its pioneering spirit by the information security industry.

Once developed, deployed, tested, and refined, this standard became one of the most important in the area of threat intelligence and information sharing. The need for this type of codification remains important to anyone tasked with managing or maintaining enterprise grade information security technologies (e.g., firewalls, IDSs, IPSs, e-mail and web gateways, malware analysis platforms or endpoint detection and response platforms, etc.), in addition to those tasked with performing forensic investigations, incident response, or threat intelligence research.

The OpenIOC standard has proven to be quite successful and widely adopted. So successful, that during the course of their incident response engagements and product roll outs Mandiant was often asked by their clients and customers whether or not they had given thought to sharing these data beyond the Mandiant platform. After some consideration a decision was made by the team at Mandiant to create the OpenIOC initiative with its community element. In doing so, Mandiant would be able to accommodate the requests of the information security community by opening the standard up beyond their tool and utilities. Mandiant brought several new tools and utilities to the market to support the adoption of this new standard while striving to communicate threat information at machine speed. The ability to deliver threat intelligence in a machine-oriented (readable) fashion at machine speed proved to be extremely well received by the information security community. Due to the ever-evolving state of the Internet threat landscape, the ability to provide robust and meaningful intelligence rapidly in a manner that is actionable is critical. Doing so aids in ensuring the swift detection, response, and approach to targeted attacks.

How It Works

The OpenIOC schema is based on an XML framework. This framework enables the user to document and categorize forensics artifacts of intrusions in an easy, lightweight manner. Furthermore, it enables those who use it to describe the technical characteristics that identify a known threat, an attacker's methodology, or other evidence of compromise.

How Do You Get It

Getting OpenIOC is easy, as there are free tools available at the official FireEye website. Tools such as the IOC Editor (which is used to create IOCs), or the Redline tool used in host-based investigations are available online for immediate use by all who seek them. The raw XML is also available at this site. Your organization can keep abreast of the latest innovations associated with OpenIOC by visiting the Mandiant's public Github site or via the OpenIOC Google Group (Fig. 4.1).

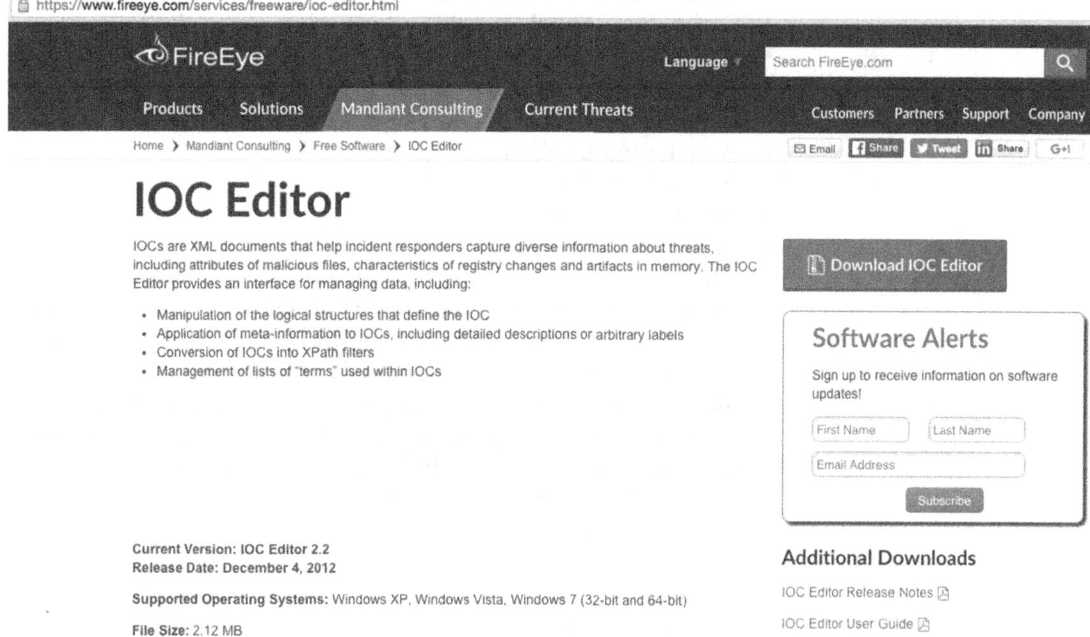

Fig. 4.1 Example of FireEye's IOC Editor Tool

Incident Object Description Exchange Format (RFC5070)

As we have seen in the previous sections, data sharing is vital to properly identifying, triaging, and mitigating threats as we encounter them within our environments. Standards such as

OpenIOC, as we have seen, enable organizations to share information specific to IOC. Beyond the adoption and use of indicator information within our enterprises, organizations may find that they require additional help from third parties to mitigate threats targeting their enterprises while seeking to gain a deeper insight and understanding into potential threats. In order to ensure that this sort of coordination can occur between disparate parties, a new standard was introduced by the IETF that promises to help represent and share data. That standard is the IODEF. It was defined by the IETF in RFC5070 as "...a format for representing computer security information commonly exchanged between Computer Security Incident Response Teams (CSIRTs)." The format provides an XML representation devised to enable the communication of incident information across and between administrative domains between parties that have an operational obligation and responsibility for remediation. According to the RFC, the data model encodes information about the following:

- Hosts
- Networks
- Services
- Attack methodology
- Forensic evidence
- Impact of the activity
- Workflow (limited)

Though the original purpose of the IODEF standard was to improve the operational capabilities of CSIRTs it is being championed beyond these organizations to organizations not tasked with the same responsibilities, namely enterprise businesses. Like all data sharing standards, adoption and ratification is taking some time; however, IODEF's community-oriented value proposition provides an improved ability to resolve incidents in a timely fashion while communicating situational awareness through collaboration and data sharing.

IODEF Data Model

The IETF has defined the IODEF data model as being a data representation, which provides a framework for sharing information commonly exchanged by CSIRTs about computer security incidents. When defining the data model, the IETF considered the following points[8]:

[8]https://www.ietf.org/rfc/rfc5070.txt

- The data model serves as a transport format and is not an optimal representation for on-disk storage, long-term archiving, or in-memory processing
- There is no precise or universally agreed upon definition of an "incident." As a result, the model does not try to dictate one through its implementation. IODEF is considered with being flexible enough to accommodate most operators
- IODEF strives to be a framework to communicate commonly exchanged incident information
- Because the domain of security analysis is not fully standardized and must rely on free-form textual descriptions, IODEF attempts to create a balance between supporting the free-form content and, at the same time, supporting and allowing automated processing of incident information
- IODEF is only one of several security-relevant data representations that are being converted into industry-accepted standards

This balanced approach to both data representation and sharing will likely encourage continued development and adoption of the IODEF standard.

IODEF Implementation

As mentioned earlier in this section, the IODEF implementation has been defined as an XML schema. This XML schema provides numerous advantages to the organizations seeking to adopt and deploy the standard. The extensibility of the schema makes it "...ideal for specifying a data encoding framework that supports various character encodings..."[9] There are many well-defined active use cases of sharing with IODEF. Many of those use cases can be found online at websites such as http://siis.realmv6.org/implementations. Use cases, tools, and open-source implementation codes can be found at this site and others like it which enable the deployment of the infrastructure necessary for the adoption of IODEF RID servers.[10]

IOCBucket.com

Another alternative to OpenIOC and IODEF for sharing IOCs is the IOCBucket. It was created by three security professionals who were active in the penetration testing industry. IOCBucket.com,

[9] https://www.ietf.org/rfc/rfc5070.txt
[10] http://siis.realmv6.org/implementations/

the site that hosts the IOCBucket exchange, provides a significant amount of information regarding their origins, their purpose, and their intent with respect to facilitating intelligent indicator sharing. It's a global community of computer and information security professionals who have what they believe to be a vested interest in sharing IOCs during their research. The owners believe that their website acts as a trans-oceanic gap between multinational corporations providing them with a wealth of incident response knowledge and experience.[11] The community thrives upon the contributions of industry OpenIOCs and aspires to be the largest repository of open source indicators in the world. The website affords users with the opportunity to check and search for IOCs found on ones network against a reputation database in order to determine the potential and possibility of infection using one of the 500 fields that are supported by the OpenIOC standard. OpenIOCs are made available for download in order for the end user to continue his or her search for infections and intrusions within his or her network. The site is not owned, operated, or sponsored by any government personnel or agencies (Fig. 4.2).

Fig. 4.2 IOCBucket.com

[11] https://www.iocbucket.com/about

Cyber Observable eXpression

CybOX is another system designed for sharing IOCs or observables for all cyber security use cases. According to its founders, it is a flexible system that supports domain-specific standards and solutions through a unified and consistent foundational definition of cyber observables.[12] In most instances utilization of CybOx should be indirect with a primary focus being on the use case domain-specific standard or solution that leverages CybOx as an enabler according to the authors. The standard adheres to the following principles for scoping of information (IOC and observable) content:

- Information content related to cyber observables is only included in CybOx if it is of general user to multiple cases and not found to be in conflict within any specific use cases
- Data regarding cyber observables that are specific to a single supported use case domain may be managed in a use case domain-specific standard or solution that leverages CybOx for all general cyber observable informational content.

Supported use cases would include things like (Table 4.3).[13]

Table 4.3 Cybox Use Cases

Supported Use Case	Relevant Process	Domain Specific Standard
Analyze event data from diverse set of sensors of different types and different vendors	Event Management	CybOX
Detect malicious activity utilizing attack patterns	Attack Detection	Common Attack Pattern Enumeration and Classification (CAPEC™)
Detect malicious activity utilizing malware behavior characterizations	Attack Detection	Malware Attribute Enumeration and Characterization (MAEC™)
Enable automated attack detection signature rule generation	Attack Detection	CybOX, MAEC, CAPEC, Structured Threat Information eXpression (STIX™)
Characterize malicious activity utilizing attack patterns	Incident Response/ Management	CAPEC, STIX
Identify new attack patterns	Threat Characterization	CAPEC
Prioritize existing attack patterns based on tactical reality	Security Testing and Secure Development	CAPEC, STIX

Continued

[12] http://cyboxproject.github.io/documentation/use-cases/

[13] http://makingsecuritymeasurable.mitre.org/docs/cybox-intro-handout.pdf

Table 4.3 Cybox Use Cases—*Cont'd*

Supported Use Case	Relevant Process	Domain Specific Standard
Characterize malware behavior	Malware Analysis	MAEC
Guide malware analysis utilizing attack patterns	Malware Analysis	MAEC, CAPEC
Detect malware effects	Attack Detection and Incident Response/ Management	Open Vulnerability and Assessment Language (OVAL®), MAEC, STIX
Enable collaborative attack indicator sharing	Information Sharing	
Empower and guide incident management utilizing attack patterns and malware characterizations	Incident Response/ Management	STIX, CAPEC, MAEC, CybOX
Enable consistent, useful and automation-capable incident alerts	Incident Response/ Management	STIX, MAEC, CAPEC
Enable automatic application of mitigations specified in attack patterns	Incident Response/ Management	STIX
Enable incident information sharing	Incident Response/ Management	STIX
Support correlation between observed properties and malicious indicators as part of digital forensics	Digital Forensics	Digital Forensics XML (DFXML), STIX, MAEC, CAPEC
Capture digital forensics analysis results	Digital Forensics	DFXML
Capture digital forensics provenance information	Digital Forensics	DFXML
Enable collaborative sharing of digital forensics information	Digital Forensics	DFXML
Enable explicit and implicit sharing controls for cyber observable information	Information Sharing	STIX, CybOX, Trusted Automated eXchange of Indicator Information (TAXII™)
Enable new levels of meta-analysis on operational cyber observables	Cyber Situational Awareness	CybOX, STIX

Summary

In this chapter we discussed the importance in being able to distinguish intelligence from information in order to ensure actionability through one of the schemas, frameworks, or standards that we introduced to the reader. We described for the reader the concepts of the IOA, IOC, and IOI. We presented the OpenIOC framework, IODEF (RFC5070), IOCBucket, and CybOx for your review and consideration paying attention to the unique detail, which comprise each of these offerings and their specialized use cases. Furthermore, this chapter was designed as an introduction to these concepts and as a prelude to more complex situations and scenarios, which will be presented in later chapters of this book.

5

KNOWLEDGE SHARING AND COMMUNITY SUPPORT

Synopsis

Threat modeling is an effective tool used to understand the threat landscape within an enterprise network. However, using data generated from within the enterprise network only allows for a partial view of the threat landscape as well as the threats potentially targeting it or the security breaches that may have already occurred. To overcome this, threat modeling, as well as threat forecasting, should be performed using knowledge elements available within community-driven threat intelligence feeds. Enterprise adoption of community sharing may initially be met with hesitation because, as is the case with most community-driven projects, sharing knowledge elements may be considered insecure and potentially a bigger risk than the advantages it could provide. To help focus on the indicator of interest or indicator of compromise (i.e., the knowledge element), most community-sharing options have been designed to only express the data needed to understand the threat.

There are multiple community sharing options currently available to enterprises. These include projects from companies like Verizon and Mandiant (a FireEye company) as well as community-driven initiatives sponsored by the United States Department of Homeland Security. Verizon offers its VERIS Framework and associated community database via a dedicated website for the project. Verizon still actively uses this project for their incident response (IR) and the generation of the annual Verizon Data Breach Investigations Report. Mandiant offers its OpenIOC framework and a base set of indicators via a dedicated website for the project. Mandiant also actively uses this project for their IR and products. Two of the most popular community-driven projects are

Threat Forecasting. http://dx.doi.org/10.1016/B978-0-12-800006-9.00005-7

the TAXII and STIX expression languages. TAXII is most commonly used as a transport mechanism for threat intelligence data including STIX as well as other similar projects. Knowledge elements are also available via commercial offerings and can be considered where they are the right fit for an enterprise. They can be complementary to community sharing feeds and do not have to be a replacement for community sharing.

The best way for enterprises to stay ahead of the adversary is to include community-driven threat intelligence feeds within their threat forecasting. The enterprise network has been expanded past the traditional brick and mortar boundary that previously existed, as enterprises expand their services into the cloud and opt for application service providers for mission critical services. This complicates the process of securing enterprise assets from exploitation and company sensitive data from exfiltration. By incorporating community sharing within threat modeling, enterprises around the world can alert each other when an attack has occurred. This allows consumers of the published knowledge elements to validate their security coverage as well as validate if a security breach has occurred.

Threat modeling, when combined with community sharing, provides the enterprise with the most holistic and near real-time view of the threat landscape allowing for better mitigation of strategies as well as faster time to detection of security breaches. This also strengthens the enterprise's knowledge when performing threat forecasting.

Introduction

The security threats facing today's enterprises present themselves through many attack vectors. These threats can be in the form of opportunistic attacks to targeted attacks as commonly seen within specific verticals like the financial industry. Regardless of the type of attack, enterprises can find themselves unprepared without proper evaluation of their threat landscape and understanding of the current threats impacting the enterprises and organizations around the world. Threat modeling is a common practice to best understand the risks and potentially identify holes within current security precautions; however, using data generated within the enterprise only gives a partial view of the risks that may exist and fails to identify potential breaches that have already occurred. This limited view also fails to identify areas within the enterprise where the kill chain needs to be mitigated based on a lack of security efficacy from the currently deployed security solutions.

Knowledge elements, in the form of indicators, should be collected from external sources to give a holistic view of the threat landscape. These knowledge elements can be from industry-specific community-driven threat intelligence feeds or from open-source threat intelligence feeds. Regardless of the source, these additional knowledge elements will improve threat modeling and give the enterprise a better view of the current threat landscape.

Sharing Knowledge Elements

One of the best ways to build accurate threat modeling and threat forecasting is through the sharing of knowledge elements. These elements can come from a variety of locations including community sourced feeds as well as through commercial subscriptions. The big question is how does an enterprise decide that it should share indicators of interest, or knowledge elements, from its own infrastructure? Sharing these data can help protect other enterprises including those within the same vertical (i.e., critical infrastructure, healthcare, finance). However, sharing this type of data may inadvertently disclose sensitive information, including intellectual properly, without the enterprise's knowledge, as well as attack data that could be used to compromise an enterprise that may not have properly resolved the current vulnerability.

To make the correct assessment, advantages, and disadvantages must be weighed. This will allow the enterprise to make the best decision. This can be done for all data points up front with the correct provisions put in place to protect any sensitive data, as well as on a per indicator basis where more scrutiny can be applied. The following sections will help outline some common advantages and disadvantages to consider.

Advantages

When preparing to share knowledge elements, there are many advantages to the enterprise that is looking to assist within its own industry-specific vertical or with the general information security community. There can be some hesitation at this concept of disclosing data considering the volume of data breaches relating to healthcare companies like Anthem, Inc.,[1,2] and retail companies

[1] Anthem Hack may have impacted millions of noncustomers as well, Newcomb, A., ABC News, online, http://abcnews.go.com/Technology/anthem-hack-impacted-millions-customers/story?id=29212840.

[2] How to access and sign up for identity theft repair and credit monitoring services, Anthem, Inc., online, https://www.anthemfacts.com/.

like Target.[3] To best understand the value of sharing these elements, it is important to review the advantages and understand how working together can help provide the most efficient protection against cyber threats.

One of the biggest advantages to sharing knowledge elements is getting access to threat vectors. To make these resources as rich with content as they are requires the participation of their user base, or community, to keep the content provided current and of value to the consumers (who are also the providers of it). Some community-based sharing does require participation from the user community (i.e., you cannot just consume, you must provide as well) to be able to access updates. This model follows some torrent-based sharing sites where ratios of upload to download are monitored. These torrent sites do this to make sure consumers of content are still providers. If not, they are denied access to new content until their upload to download ratio has returned to within community standards.

The next advantage to highlight is that of building a collection of recent knowledge elements from external sources. Once collection of knowledge elements begins, an enterprise can potentially get an advantage over the threat actors. There may be a percentage of overlap in knowledge elements; however, these can be discarded in favor of unique elements or ones not yet seen according to the enterprise's collection procedures and practices. All knowledge elements, whether collected by the enterprise or through a shared resource, can help an enterprise best identify weaknesses in their threat landscape when performing threat forecasting. Once these weaknesses are identified, proper action can be taken to either patch potential targets before these become the victim of or pivot point[4] in a larger planned attack or updating security solutions (i.e., NGFW, NGIPS, WAF, AV) to mitigate the kill chain.

The last main advantage to highlight is that of assisting others within the community. Coordinated attacks target specific industry verticals, including crimeware kits and types of malware, and working with other enterprises within the same vertical will provide a great vantage point within the cyber security domain. Enterprises can see the type of threats targeting them today as well as those they may be target with in the near future. This is all made possible through the sharing of knowledge elements. Referencing

[3]Target puts data breach costs at $148 million, and forecasts drop profit, Abrams, R. New York Times, online, http://www.nytimes.com/2014/08/06/business/target-puts-data-breach-costs-at-148-million.html?_r=0.

[4]Metaploit unleashed—pivoting, offensive security, online, http://www.offensive-security.com/metasploit-unleashed/Pivoting.

the earlier example of the Anthem breach, community sharing within The National Healthcare Information Sharing and Analysis Center (NH-ISAC) leveraging community driven TAXII and STIX expression languages (refer to the Community Sharing section for more information on TAXII and STIX), NH-ISAC was able to confirm within 60 minutes the extent of the breach as well as who else may have been targeted and subsequently breached.[5] This was made possible by the NH-ISAC's National Health Cybersecurity Intelligence System providing security intelligence to its members including the Indicators of Compromise (IOC), or knowledge elements, which allowed these members to report whether or not they had seen them within their enterprise networks. This example highlights the benefits of community sharing as the healthcare vertical came together, shared knowledge elements within its vertical, identified the impact to the user community across multiple enterprises and, within a relatively short amount of time, determined the span of a very large attack across this industry.

Knowledge is power.

Disadvantages

There are many advantages to sharing knowledge elements within an enterprise-specific vertical or with the greater information-security community. There are, though, some disadvantages that should be considered prior to jumping in with both feet. Each enterprise may experience its own unique challenges when sharing knowledge elements. These may stem from internal politics, infrastructure challenges, or a lack of understanding of the benefits associated with sharing within a trusted community. Most disadvantages can be overcome when properly planned for and need not be reasons for not sharing knowledge elements.

The first disadvantage is exposing your enterprise network attack data to third parties (which may include other enterprises with whom there is no trust relationship). Shared data, if examined, may allow a consumer of said data to determine if the enterprise producing the data has been compromised. An enterprise may choose to share knowledge elements that are directly related to a data breach knowing they have not fully remediated all potential vulnerable components within their enterprise network. This decision is made to allow others within the same industry vertical or within the same sharing community to prepare for a similar

[5]The National Health ISAC (NH-ISAC) 60-min. response to the Anthem Attack, NH-ISAC, online, http://www.nhisac.org/blog/the-national-health-isac-nh-isac-60-minute-response-to-the-anthem-attack/.

attack or confirm they have not experienced the same compromise of their enterprise networks. What would happen if someone with nefarious intentions was monitoring where you, as this compromised enterprise, post knowledge elements including IOCs? This person may have confirmation that a specific threat vector was successful in compromising your enterprise network. Furthermore, it may give them insight into your threat landscape. By sharing knowledge elements, you may be opening yourself up to additional attacks from threat actors who are using this information for nefarious purposes.

The next disadvantage is time-to-release information. Knowledge elements, including those that are built from items such as IOCs, are needed by IR teams within a time window for them to be of most use. Producers of knowledge elements, who are concerned about their misuse, as outlined previously, may hold on to or delay reporting information from within their enterprise network so that their sharing is not used against them. This time delay, whether it is measured in hours, days or even weeks, would allow the producer of the knowledge elements to patch all vulnerable points (or configure mitigation via their security products) within their enterprise network prior to releasing any shared content. This would allow the producer to protect themselves while still contributing to the community. However, based on the rate at which attacks can propagate through the Internet, as well as how orchestrated attacks may hit multiple victims within days of each other, time to release of these knowledge elements is critical to success in the community sharing model.

The last main disadvantage to sharing knowledge elements is the sanitization of the content being shared. Producers of knowledge elements may want to sanitize all content being produced prior to release into the shared community. The goal of this sanitization may be to protect company-sensitive information, including customer data as well as company intellectual property. For whatever the reason, sanitization may be a step in generating knowledge elements. Sanitization of data, whether performed through automation or a manual process, could potentially slow down the generation and distribution of knowledge elements. This could also, depending on how much data has been sanitized, make the knowledge elements being shared of no value to the community. Delayed knowledge elements sanitized to the point of no value does not help the information security to better protect against malicious attacks.

There may be additional disadvantages that are not covered within this section as its goal is not to be fully comprehensive as to every challenge an enterprise may face. The goal is to highlight several of the main concerns raised by enterprises and discuss solutions. Knowledge elements, whether directly used as IOCs or as Indicators of Interests, are designed to be elements that can be uniquely mapped to a threat vector such that it can help both enterprises and IR teams to identify malicious patterns within network communications within an endpoint. These indicators are usually designed, as will be outlined within Community Sharing, to include specific, measurable data and not enterprise-sensitive information. Knowledge elements are items such as URLs, public IP addresses (not related to the enterprise) and cryptographic hash values for known bad content. In general, these data do not relate to the three main disadvantages outlined. An enterprise would be able to publish this content without needing to sanitize. Furthermore, as knowledge elements are highly focused content, enterprises can publish this content as quickly as they can process it. This allows for maximum protection within the community in which this content is shared. Finally, sharing within a trusted community, such as the enterprise's industry vertical, will help with the concern that shared content could turn into a source of reconnaissance for the threat actor. This is highlighted within the example of Anthem and NH-ISAC.

Community Sharing

When researching sources for knowledge elements, there are several possibilities available, including community sharing and commercial offerings. Prior to looking at or in addition to supplementing commercial offerings, organizations should explore community sharing. Community sharing options range from projects that were defined within IR companies that have migrated to the community, to projects that initially started within the community. Regardless of how the sharing originated, the goal today is to provide access to threat intelligence so that action can be taken by an enterprise to update its security measures before it is compromised, as well as to identify if a compromise has already occurred.

This section outlines several of the community sharing options available at the writing of this book. This list is not meant to be exhaustive or complete; however, the following options are commonly discussed within the security intelligence community. Each have their own unique components based on how they were developed and introduced to the community. There is no reason why multiple community feeds cannot be combined together for maximum coverage nor is there any reason why community feeds cannot be combined with commercial offerings. However, for community sharing to be the most effective, consumers of the community feeds should also be producers of content and contribute any knowledge elements detected within their own networks.

VERIS

The Vocabulary for Event Recording and Incident Sharing, or VERIS, is a community project started by the Verizon RISK (Research, Investigations, Solutions, Knowledge) Team. Initially, VERIS was launched by the Verizon IR Team as a way to present the aggregated results collected during their investigations for the annual Verizon Data Breach Investigations Report (DBIR) and was used by them as early as the 2010 DBIR. VERIS was initially branded the Verizon Enterprise Reporting and Incident Sharing framework and later rebranded to its current name when the framework became available to the information security community. Today, Verizon provides it, via its own website,[6] as a way to express metrics in a common format for describing security events. VERIS has several objectives. The first is to build a community of users who can compile a library of quality security information and share this information, anonymously and responsibly, with others within this community. The second is to build a foundation for the community to learn from each other's experiences to best measure and manage risk. The final objective is to provide organizations with the tools needed to get started, including how to leverage it within the organization, how to interact with the community and how to build a valuable set of information that benefits all.

The VERIS framework was designed to address an issue, perceived by its creators, where the lack of widespread participation and community activity was, in part, due to a lack of adoption of a commonly used taxonomy. VERIS was designed to be a set of metrics that provided a common language for articulating security events in a detailed and repeatable manner in such a way as to encourage constructive and cooperative sharing. This allows all members of the community to learn from one another's experiences to best manage security posture and risk. The VERIS community website discusses domain of information risk as being four overlapping landscapes identified as Asset, Control, Impact, and Threat. This is visually shown in the following Venn diagram

[6]VERIS—the vocabulary for event recording and incident sharing, VERIS Community (and Verizon RISK Team), online, http://veriscommunity.net/.

(Fig. 5.1[7]). An enterprise's capability to understand and manage risk requires information from each of these four landscapes. VERIS uses this as its foundation and leverages these data, along with the four A's (actor, actions, assets, attributes), into its schema, which is built off the examination of breach data and postincident analysis. This provides security metrics that create knowledge elements that improve the enterprise's ability to make decisions based on data.

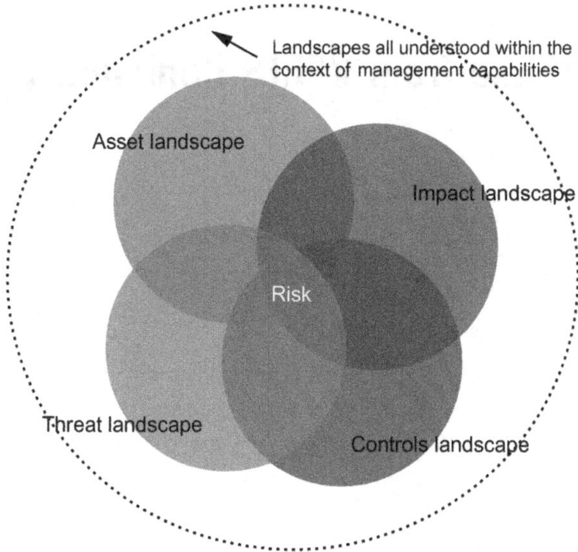

Fig. 5.1 VERIS venn diagram.

The VERIS framework schema is comprised of five sections. Each section includes items unique to its section to better help define the security event. The goal of this schema is to provide the enterprise with information that can help to determine the cause and measure the severity. The goal, however, is not to collect every last bit of data related to the security event. The VERIS framework has the intent to provide actionable data without needing to provide completeness. The five main sections that make up the VERIS framework are incident tracking, victim demographics, IR, discovery and response, and impact assessment.

[7]VERIS Venn Diagram, VERIS Community (and Verizon RISK Team), online, http://veriscommunity.net/veris-overview.html.

As at the time of writing, the current version of the VERIS framework defines objects using JSON.[8] Example 1[9] includes a JSON classification from the VERIS website outlining a single incident in which a company sensitive document was emailed to a personal email address. VERIS supports a community database, the VERIS Community Database (VCDB), which is available online. It includes updates from the Verizon RISK Team where data can be anonymized along with support from the VERIS community.

Example 1 Email Abuse from VERIS Community


```
{
  "action": {
    "misuse": {
      "variety": [
        "Email misuse"
      ],
      "vector": [
        "LAN access"
      ]
    }
  },
  "actor": {
    "internal": {
      "motive": [
        "Convenience"
      ],
      "variety": [
        "End user"
      ]
    }
  },
  "asset": {
    "assets": [
      {
```


[8]Introducing JSON, online, http://json.org/.
[9]Email abuse, VERIS Community (and Verizon RISK Team), online, http://veriscommunity.net/class-examples.html#section-email-abuse.

```
                "variety": "U - Desktop"
            }
        ],
        "ownership": "Victim"
    },
    "attribute": {
        "confidentiality": {
            "data_disclosure": "Potentially"
        }
    },
    "reference": "http://youtu.be/WhWavua-1FI",
    "victim": [
        {
            "country": "US",
            "employee_count": "100 to 1000",
            "industry": "515210",
            "state": "NY",
            "victim_id": "Plaza Cable"
        }
    ]
}
```


The VERIS framework and the VERIS Community Database are both available on GitHub. Both are active projects as at the time of writing.

- VERIS Framework—https://github.com/vz-risk/veris
- VERISCommunityDatabase—https://github.com/vz-risk/VCDB.

OpenIOC

The Open Indictors of Compromise (OpenIOC) is an open source framework developed by Mandiant (now a FireEye Company) for sharing threat intelligence. Much like VERIS, the OpenIOC framework started as an internal project at Mandiant for the purpose of letting its products and services rapidly search through intelligence collected to help quickly identify security breaches. Mandiant's goal was to build a schema that allowed them (and subsequently the community) to be able to describe the components of a threat, an attack methodology or any evidence of a compromise and provide a way to share this threat intelligence, as well as digest this intelligence, as quickly as possible. For this reason, Mandiant built the OpenIOC framework as an extensible XML schema that could be easily machine-digestible. This would allow for faster dissemination of threat information to the community.

The OpenIOC framework, along with its supporting tools, was created to address the perceived issue that threat metrics could not be shared between organizations or between groups within the same organization quick enough to handle the rate at which an attacker may transition from target to target. Critical data needed to be passed in a format that could be machine-digestible so that action could be taken within a shorter time-frame, limiting the window of exposure. Also, this critical data needed to be put into an industry-accepted format so that it would allow the contained information to be easily digestible giving the consumer multiple options for processing it. Building upon an industry-accepted format, this critical data needed to also be in an extensible language so that new entries, or indicators, can be lightweight and small as well as being able to be customized (i.e., extended) to fit the needs of the item being reported. Finally, putting the OpenIOC into XML allows easy conversion into other formats, such as JSON (as the VERIS Framework uses). The XML schema and certain indicator terms have been released under the Apache 2 license.[10]

IOCs are a critical part of most IR programs. Mandiant defines their IR process in *An Introduction to OpenIOC*[11] and is outlined in Fig. 5.2. For a framework like OpenIOC to be successful, IOCs must be examined and reexamined throughout the IR lifecycle. This is similar to when this framework is used for threat modeling (outside of responding to an incident within the enterprise network). IOC creation is based on an event containing data relating to an attack, malware modifications or some other attacker driven data point. Once all IOCs are created based on collected data, they can be deployed throughout an enterprise network to help drive awareness of other systems that could be compromised. Any suspicious machines identified within the enterprise network can be evaluated for additional knowledge elements, or IOCs, including modifications to the system, log data, and network access. Once these data have been reviewed, IOCs that have been deployed

[10]Apache License Version 2.0, The Apache Software Foundation, Online, http://www.apache.org/licenses/LICENSE-2.0.

[11]An introduction to OpenIOC, OpenIOC Framework (Mandiant, Inc.), White Paper (online), http://openioc.org/resources/An_Introduction_to_OpenIOC.pdf.

can be updated, where needed, and new ones can be generated to assist in identifying the full impact of the attack. All IOCs, new and updated, are deployed/redeployed and the process continues.

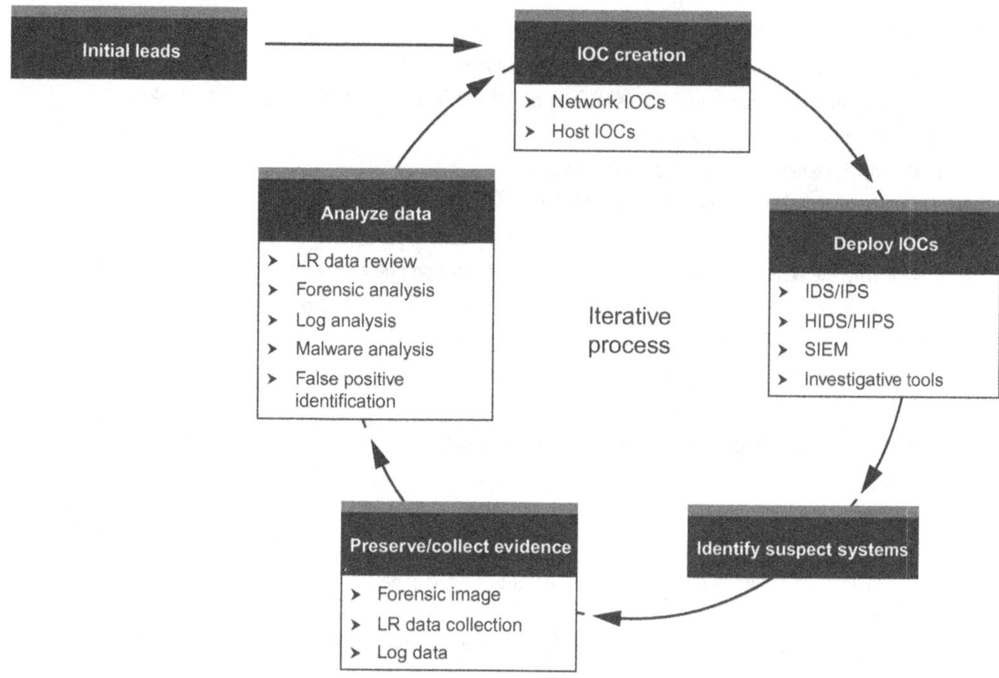

Fig. 5.2 Create and refine IOCs.[10]

The direct usage of the OpenIOC and its original purpose for creation is assistance with IR. This does not mean it cannot serve additional purposes. IOCs are other forms of knowledge elements and can be used to assist with threat modeling. Sharing of knowledge within the OpenIOC framework within the information security community can help organizations and enterprises properly leverage knowledge elements to measure the impact to their current threat landscape, as well as to guide decisions and predict future risk. Example 2[12] outlines Stuxnet using the OpenIOC indictor structure and is one of the few examples available on the OpenIOC website. As outlined, the structure is in XML and includes Mandiant's "Virus Methodology" for Stuxnet.

[12]IOC example: Stuxnet, OpenIOC Framework (Mandiant, Inc.), online, http://openioc.org/iocs/ea3cab0c-72ad-40cc-abbf-90846fa4afec.ioc.

Example 2 IOC Example: Stuxnet from OpenIOC website

```
<?xml version="1.0" encoding="us-ascii"?>
<ioc xmlns:xsi="http://www.w3.org/2001/XMLSchema-instance"
xmlns:xsd="http://www.w3.org/2001/XMLSchema" id="ea3cab0c-72ad-40cc-abbf-90846fa4afec"
last-modified="2011-11-04T19:35:05"
xmlns="http://schemas.mandiant.com/2010/ioc">
  <short_description>STUXNET VIRUS (METHODOLOGY)</short_description>
  <description>Generic indicator for the stuxnet virus. When loaded, stuxnet spawns lsass.exe in a suspended
  state. The malware then maps in its own executable section and fixes up the CONTEXT to point to the newly
  mapped in section. This is a common task performed by malware and allows the malware to execute under the
  pretense of a known and trusted process.</description>
  <keywords>methodology</keywords>
  <authored_by>Mandiant</authored_by>
  <authored_date>0001-01-01T00:00:00</authored_date>
  <links />
  <definition>
   <Indicator operator="OR" id="73bc8d65-826b-48d2-b4a8-48918e29e323">
    <IndicatorItem id="b9ef2559-cc59-4463-81d9-52800545e16e"
  condition="contains">
     <Context document="FileItem" search="FileItem/PEInfo/Sections/Section/Name"
  type="mir" />
     <Content type="string">.stub</Content>
    </IndicatorItem>
    <IndicatorItem id="156bc4b6-a2a1-4735-bfe8-6c8d1f7eae38" condition="contains">
     <Context document="FileItem" search="FileItem/FileName" type="mir" />
     <Content type="string">mdmcpq3.PNF</Content>
    </IndicatorItem>
    <IndicatorItem id="e57d9a5b-5e6a-41ec-87c8-ee67f3ed2e20" condition="contains">
     <Context document="FileItem" search="FileItem/FileName" type="mir" />
     <Content type="string">mdmeric3.PNF</Content>
    </IndicatorItem>
    <IndicatorItem id="63d7bee6-b575-4d56-8d43-1c5eac57658f"
  condition="contains">
     <Context document="FileItem" search="FileItem/FileName" type="mir" />
     <Content type="string">oem6C.PNF</Content>
    </IndicatorItem>
    <IndicatorItem id="e6bff12a-e23d-45ea-94bd-8289f806bea7" condition="contains">
     <Context document="FileItem" search="FileItem/FileName" type="mir" />
```

```
      <Content type="string">oem7A.PNF</Content>
    </IndicatorItem>
    <Indicator operator="AND" id="422ae9bf-a1ae-41f2-8e54-5b4c6f3e1598">
      <IndicatorItem id="e93f1610-daaf-4311-bcf3-3aecef8271c0" condition="contains">
        <Context document="DriverItem"
search="DriverItem/DeviceItem/AttachedToDriverName" type="mir" />
        <Content type="string">fs_rec.sys</Content>
      </IndicatorItem>
      <IndicatorItem id="72476f35-8dea-4bae-8239-7c22d05d664f"
condition="contains">
        <Context document="DriverItem"
search="DriverItem/DeviceItem/AttachedToDriverName" type="mir" />
        <Content type="string">mrxsmb.sys</Content>
      </IndicatorItem>
      <IndicatorItem id="f98ea5aa-9e23-4f18-b871-b3cf5ba153fe" condition="contains">
        <Context document="DriverItem"
search="DriverItem/DeviceItem/AttachedToDriverName" type="mir" />
        <Content type="string">sr.sys</Content>
      </IndicatorItem>
      <IndicatorItem id="32f61140-0f58-43bc-8cdd-a25db75ca6c4"
condition="contains">
        <Context document="DriverItem"
search="DriverItem/DeviceItem/AttachedToDriverName" type="mir" />
        <Content type="string">fastfat.sys</Content>
      </IndicatorItem>
    </Indicator>
    <Indicator operator="AND" id="eb585bf5-18d8-4837-baf0-80ac74104ca3">
      <IndicatorItem id="8d85b559-4d18-4e15-b0c9-da5a9b32f53c"
condition="contains">
        <Context document="FileItem" search="FileItem/FileName" type="mir" />
        <Content type="string">mrxcls.sys</Content>
      </IndicatorItem>
      <IndicatorItem id="8a3e425d-fa87-4a31-b20d-8f8630d77933"
condition="contains">
        <Context document="FileItem"
search="FileItem/PEInfo/DigitalSignature/CertificateSubject" type="mir" />
        <Content type="string">Realtek Semiconductor Corp</Content>
      </IndicatorItem>
    </Indicator>
    <Indicator operator="AND" id="bc8d06dd-f879-4609-bb1c-eccded0222ce">
```

```
<IndicatorItem id="89f194d3-3ee6-4218-93f8-055ea92a9f00"
condition="contains">
   <Context document="FileItem" search="FileItem/FileName" type="mir" />
   <Content type="string">mrxnet.sys</Content>
  </IndicatorItem>
  <IndicatorItem id="c2dae8bf-81b1-49fb-8654-396830d75ade"
condition="contains">
   <Context document="FileItem"
search="FileItem/PEInfo/DigitalSignature/CertificateSubject" type="mir" />
   <Content type="string">Realtek Semiconductor Corp</Content>
  </IndicatorItem>
  </Indicator>
  <Indicator operator="AND" id="00538c36-88fe-42ea-a70f-136a2fb53834">
  <IndicatorItem id="a779b811-345f-4164-897e-0752837d0c1e"
condition="contains">
   <Context document="RegistryItem" search="RegistryItem/Path" type="mir" />
   <Content
type="string">HKEY_LOCAL_MACHINE\SYSTEM\ControlSet001\Services\MRxCls\ImagePath</Content>
  </IndicatorItem>
  <IndicatorItem id="ee981f06-b713-40aa-ac98-c6f4fd82b78d"
condition="contains">
   <Context document="RegistryItem" search="RegistryItem/Text" type="mir" />
   <Content type="string">mrxcls.sys</Content>
  </IndicatorItem>
  </Indicator>
  <Indicator operator="AND" id="d8d9b32c-f648-4552-9805-93c05ed48219">
  <IndicatorItem id="c08044e7-e88c-433c-b463-763bdddeff82"
condition="contains">
   <Context document="RegistryItem" search="RegistryItem/Path" type="mir" />
   <Content
type="string">HKEY_LOCAL_MACHINE\SYSTEM\ControlSet001\Services\MRxNet\ImagePath</Content>
  </IndicatorItem>
  <IndicatorItem id="38dfb382-ebbe-4685-bbb7-60675b91bd15"
condition="contains">
   <Context document="RegistryItem" search="RegistryItem/Text" type="mir" />
   <Content type="string">mrxnet.sys</Content>
  </IndicatorItem>
  </Indicator>
 </Indicator>
 </definition>
</ioc>
```

The OpenIOC framework, along with a set of indicators, is available on the OpenIOC website:

- OpenIOC Framework—http://www.openioc.org.

TAXII

The Trusted Automated eXchange of Indicator Information, or TAXII, is a community-driven effort to automate the exchange of trusted threat intelligence. The office of Cybersecurity and Communications at the United States Department of Homeland Security (DHS) sponsors and leads the effort within the community. The MITRE Corporation, a nonprofit organization, has copyrighted all the specifications in an effort to keep it an open standard that can be leveraged by enterprises, government agencies, and security vendors. This effort was initially launched in early 2013 with the Draft-1 of Version 1.0 of the TAXII specifications[13] and was followed by the official release of Version 1.0 at the beginning of 2014.[13] As at the time of writing, the TAXII specifications are at Version 1.1.

TAXII is an XML structured framework and the specifications outline how messages should be structured, how messages should be exchanged and what protocols should be used to transport the messages. TAXII is designed to use HTTP (or HTTPS) as its communication protocol to exchange request and response messages structured in XML. Example 3[14] and Example 4[15] outline subscription management request and response messages using TAXII Version 1.1. As TAXII is designed to be a way to exchange threat intelligence, several other efforts leverage its communication structure and are delivered as "payloads"[16] including the Structured Threat Information Expression or STIX. To participate in the TAXII community, enterprises can access the Community section of the TAXII website where they can register to receive announcements as well as related newsletters. The Community section of the website also includes a TAXII Test Server as well as several utilities to help new members get up and running as

[13]Release archive, Trusted Automated eXchange of Indicator Information, online, https://taxii.mitre.org/specifications/archive.html.

[14]Sample TAXII 1.1 collection subscription management request, Trusted Automated eXchange of Indicator Information, online, http://taxiiproject.github.io/documentation/sample-use/.

[15]Sample TAXII 1.1 collection subscription management response, Trusted Automated eXchange of Indicator Information, online, http://taxiiproject.github.io/documentation/sample-use/.

[16]Relationships to other efforts, Trusted Automated eXchange of Indicator Information, online, https://taxii.mitre.org/about/faqs.html.

easily as possible. Enterprises can look within their own industry vertical for TAXII servers providing threat intelligence unique to their vertical. There are also public servers available in which organizations can share and receive threat intelligence. An example of this is HailaTAXII.com that provides a list of available open source feeds providing threat intelligence in STIX format.[17]

Example 3 Sample TAXII 1.1 Collection Subscription Management Request

```
<taxii_11:Subscription_Management_Request
  xmlns:taxii_11="http://taxii.mitre.org/messages/taxii_xml_binding-1.1"
   message_id="96485"
   collection_name="default"
   action="SUBSCRIBE">
   <taxii_11:Subscription_Parameters>
     <taxii_11:Response_Type>FULL</taxii_11:Response_Type>
   </taxii_11:Subscription_Parameters>
</taxii_11:Subscription_Management_Request>
```

Example 4 Sample TAXII 1.1 Collection Subscription Management Response

```
<taxii_11:Subscription_Management_Response
xmlns:taxii_11="http://taxii.mitre.org/messages/taxii_xml_binding-1.1"
message_id="58469" in_response_to="96485" collection_name="default">
  <taxii_11:Subscription status="ACTIVE">
    <taxii_11:Subscription_ID>Subscription001</taxii_11:Subscription_ID>
  </taxii_11:Subscription>
</taxii_11:Subscription_Management_Response>
```

The TAXII specifications as well as information about how to join the community and other related community-driven efforts are located on the following websites.

[17]Hail a TAXII.com, online, http://hailataxii.com.

- TAXII website—https://taxii.mitre.org
- TAXII Community—http://taxii.mitre.org/community/
- TAXII Github Repository—http://taxiiproject.github.io.

STIX

The Structured Threat Information eXpression, or STIX, is an XML structured language for expressing and sharing threat intelligence. Like TAXII, STIX is a community-driven project currently led and sponsored by the office of Cybersecurity and Communications at the United States DHS. The MITRE Corporation has also copyrighted the STIX expression language in an effort to keep it an open standard that can be leveraged by enterprises, government agencies and security vendors. STIX was first defined publicly with Version 0.3 in September 2012.[18] As at the time of writing, STIX is currently at Version 1.1.1.[19] As mentioned earlier, STIX leverages TAXII as its transport mechanism such that it is delivered as part of the TAXII "payload."

STIX was designed with several guiding principles[20] in mind. The first guiding principle was being able to provide coverage across the entire cyber security domain by providing full expressivity for reporting knowledge elements. The second guiding principle was to integrate, either directly or loosely, with other threat intelligence expression languages. This includes projects like Cyber Observable eXpression (CybOX),[21] Common Attack Pattern Enumeration and Classification (CAPEC)[22] and Malware Attribute Enumeration and Characterization (MAEC).[23] The third guiding principle was to provide as much flexibility as possible in what portions of the standardized language representation are required to be included in reporting a knowledge element. The fourth guiding principle revolves around extensibility of the design of the STIX language allowing for extension mechanisms for domain-specific use, localized use or for user-driven refinement/evolution. The fifth guiding principle focused on supporting automation through maximizing structure and

[18] Release archive, structured threat information expression, online, http://stix.mitre.org/language/archive/.

[19] Version 1.1.1 official, structured threat information expression, online, http://stix.mitre.org/language/version1.1.1/.

[20] Standardizing cyber threat intelligence information with the Structured Threat Information eXpression (STIX), structured threat information expression, online, http://stixproject.github.io/getting-started/whitepaper/.

[21] Cyber Observable eXpression (CybOX), online, http://cybox.mitre.org.

[22] Common Attack Pattern Enumeration and Classification (CAPEC), online, http://capec.mitre.org.

[23] Malware Attribute Enumeration and Characterization (MAEC), online, http://maec.mitre.org.

Example 5 Sample from FireEye Poison Ivy Report

```
<stix:Indicator timestamp="2014-02-20T09:00:00.000000Z" id="fireeye:indicator-f8997797-c779-4fb0-98b0-
42e52bac422e" xsi:type="indicator:IndicatorType">
        <indicator:Title>Mutex: 1vvb8888d</indicator:Title>
        <indicator:Type xsi:type="stixVocabs:IndicatorTypeVocab-1.1">Malware Artifacts</indicator:Type>
        <indicator:Observable idref="fireeye:observable-c9252382-c1c4-42d8-9cad-9271954cb9fc"/>
        <indicator:Indicated_TTP>
            <stixCommon:TTP idref="fireeye:ttp-0be8fa38-6ca3-4f87-bf47-44e5bbf6550b"/>
        </indicator:Indicated_TTP>
        <indicator:Suggested_COAs>
            <indicator:Suggested_COA>
                <stixCommon:Course_Of_Action idref="fireeye:courseofaction-70b3d5f6-374b-4488-8688-
729b6eedac5b"/>
            </indicator:Suggested_COA>
        </indicator:Suggested_COAs>
    </stix:Indicator>
    <stix:Indicator timestamp="2014-02-20T09:00:00.000000Z" id="fireeye:indicator-0a940e60-6418-4408-9cb4-
8b293d5bcc18" xsi:type="indicator:IndicatorType">
        <indicator:Title>ID: nasa.xxuz.com</indicator:Title>
        <indicator:Type xsi:type="stixVocabs:IndicatorTypeVocab-1.1">Malware Artifacts</indicator:Type>
        <indicator:Observable idref="fireeye:observable-291b7e45-887d-4042-9345-a7ebbc5122d4"/>
        <indicator:Indicated_TTP>
            <stixCommon:TTP idref="fireeye:ttp-0be8fa38-6ca3-4f87-bf47-44e5bbf6550b"/>
        </indicator:Indicated_TTP>
        <indicator:Suggested_COAs>
            <indicator:Suggested_COA>
                <stixCommon:Course_Of_Action idref="fireeye:courseofaction-70b3d5f6-374b-4488-8688-
729b6eedac5b"/>
            </indicator:Suggested_COA>
        </indicator:Suggested_COAs>
    </stix:Indicator>
    <stix:Indicator timestamp="2014-02-20T09:00:00.000000Z" id="fireeye:indicator-927316d9-809b-4c61-96fc-
ce8573e422df" xsi:type="indicator:IndicatorType">
        <indicator:Title>Mutex: ((*HKG^%3</indicator:Title>
        <indicator:Type xsi:type="stixVocabs:IndicatorTypeVocab-1.1">Malware Artifacts</indicator:Type>
        <indicator:Observable idref="fireeye:observable-1aeb5196-3707-44fb-ae13-8b39d43204d9"/>
        <indicator:Indicated_TTP>
            <stixCommon:TTP idref="fireeye:ttp-4406c7c7-6c58-478d-aacc-0334929ebdde"/>
        </indicator:Indicated_TTP>
        <indicator:Suggested_COAs>
```

```
        <indicator:Suggested_COA>
            <stixCommon:Course_Of_Action idref="fireeye:courseofaction-70b3d5f6-374b-4488-8688-
729b6eedac5b"/>
        </indicator:Suggested_COA>
    </indicator:Suggested_COAs>
</stix:Indicator>
```

consistency. The last guiding principle was the inverse to the fifth; however, it was just as important that STIX language was human-readable as well. Human readability was considered important for early adoption as well as sustained use.

Example 5[24] outlines a sample of the STIX expression language in use within a FireEye report. This sample is outlining several indicators of Poison Ivy, a remote access tool, which gives threat actors or hackers remote access to computers and has been used in several high-profile malware campaigns.[25]

The STIX expression language, as well as information about how to join the community and access to the project repositories, is located on the following websites:

- STIX website—http://stix.mitre.org
- STIX Community—http://stix.mitre.org/community/
- STIX Github Repository—https://github.com/STIXProject/.

CybOX

The Cyber Observable eXpression, or CybOX, is an XML structured language for expressing cyber observables seen within the cyber domain or patterns that could be seen within the cyber domain. Cyber observables can be defined from a variety of events giving CybOX coverage across a large percentage of the cyber domain. CybOX can express events within threat assessments and IRs, define malware and exploit characterization, as well as assist with indicator sharing. Like TAXII and STIX, CybOX is a community-driven project currently sponsored by the office of Cybersecurity and Communications at the United States DHS.

[24] Sample from FireEye Poison Ivy report, structured threat information expression, online, https://stix.mitre.org/language/version1.1/samples/poison_ivy-stix-1.1.zip.
[25] Poison Ivy: assessing damage and extracting intelligence, FireEye, online, https://www.fireeye.com/blog/threat-research/2013/08/pivy-assessing-damage-and-extracting-intel.html.

The MITRE Corporation has also copyrighted the CybOX language in an effort to keep it an open standard that can be leveraged by enterprises, government agencies and security vendors. CybOX was first defined and released publicly with Version 0.6 in October 2011.[26] As at the time of writing, CybOX is currently at Version 2.1.[27]

In its simplest form, CybOX is an observable set of properties or characteristics that express the observation of an event within the cyber domain.[28] This can include events like changes to a file or a network event. As at the time of writing, CybOX includes a list of predefined object representations including File, HTTP Session, System, Win Computer Account, and X509 Certificate.[29] All of the predefined objects are defined within the two schemas, CybOX_Core and CybOX_Common, included with CybOX. Users who need to add additional objects to be able to define their observable within the CybOX language can add additional objects by extending the schema. This can be done within a private sharing community (i.e., within an enterprise); however, it is encouraged that this is actually done within the larger CybOX community. New object schemas can be shared on the CybOX Community Email Distribution List to allow it to be reviewed and vetted. Once it is properly vetted, it can be moved into the core CybOX distribution so the whole community can leverage it. As previously discussed, STIX was designed to leverage other threat intelligence languages. CybOX is one of these languages. STIX leverages CybOX for expressing cyber observables including patterns for use within indicators and network communications. The CybOX language schema is natively supported within the STIX language schema for this reason. Due to the relationship CybOX and STIX have, TAXII also has indirect native support for CybOX.

Example 6[30] outlines an HTTP session expressed using CybOX and is taken from the CybOX website.[30] The XML structured

[26]Release archive, Cyber Observable eXpression, online, http://cybox.mitre.org/language/archive/.
[27]Version 2.1 (official), Cyber Observable eXpression, online, http://cybox.mitre.org/language/version2.1/.
[28]CybOX language, Cyber Observable eXpression, online, http://cybox.mitre.org/about/faqs.html#B1.
[29]Which objects currently have representations defined in CybOX?, Cyber Observable eXpression, online, http://cybox.mitre.org/about/faqs.html#B2.
[30]Samples (from Version 2.1 (Official)), Cyber Observable eXpression, online, http://cybox.mitre.org/language/version2.1/#samples.

Example 6 CybOX_Network_Connection_HTTP_Instance.xml Sample from CybOX website

```
<cybox:Observables xmlns:xsi="http://www.w3.org/2001/XMLSchema-instance"
  xmlns:cybox="http://cybox.mitre.org/cybox-2"
  xmlns:cyboxCommon="http://cybox.mitre.org/common-2"
  xmlns:AddressObj="http://cybox.mitre.org/objects#AddressObject-2"
  xmlns:PortObj="http://cybox.mitre.org/objects#PortObject-2"
  xmlns:SocketAddressObj="http://cybox.mitre.org/objects#SocketAddressObject-1"
  xmlns:NetworkConnectionObj="http://cybox.mitre.org/objects#NetworkConnectionObject-2"
  xmlns:HTTPSessionObj="http://cybox.mitre.org/objects#HTTPSessionObject-2"
  xmlns:example="http://example.com/"
  xsi:schemaLocation="http://cybox.mitre.org/cybox-2
  http://cybox.mitre.org/XMLSchema/core/2.1/cybox_core.xsd
  http://cybox.mitre.org/objects#NetworkConnectionObject-2
 http://cybox.mitre.org/XMLSchema/objects/Network_Connection/2.1/Network_Connection_Object.xsd
" cybox_major_version="2" cybox_minor_version="1" cybox_update_version="0">
    <cybox:Observable id="example:Observable-1b427720-98d7-4735-b125-754c7e08f285">
      <cybox:Description>
        This Observable specifies an example instance of a Network Connection Object with an HTTP Session.
      </cybox:Description>
      <cybox:Object id="example:Object-d1fdd983-530b-489f-9ab8-ed3cb5212c35">
        <cybox:Properties
xsi:type="NetworkConnectionObj:NetworkConnectionObjectType">
          <NetworkConnectionObj:Layer3_Protocol
datatype="string">IPv4</NetworkConnectionObj:Layer3_Protocol>
          <NetworkConnectionObj:Layer4_Protocol
datatype="string">TCP</NetworkConnectionObj:Layer4_Protocol>
          <NetworkConnectionObj:Layer7_Protocol
datatype="string">HTTP</NetworkConnectionObj:Layer7_Protocol>
          <NetworkConnectionObj:Source_Socket_Address>
            <SocketAddressObj:IP_Address>

<AddressObj:Address_Value>192.168.1.15</AddressObj:Address_Value>
            </SocketAddressObj:IP_Address>
            <SocketAddressObj:Port>
              <PortObj:Port_Value>5525</PortObj:Port_Value>
            </SocketAddressObj:Port>
          </NetworkConnectionObj:Source_Socket_Address>
```

```
        <NetworkConnectionObj:Destination_Socket_Address>
          <SocketAddressObj:IP_Address>

<AddressObj:Address_Value>198.49.123.10</AddressObj:Address_Value>
          </SocketAddressObj:IP_Address>
          <SocketAddressObj:Port>
            <PortObj:Port_Value>80</PortObj:Port_Value>
          </SocketAddressObj:Port>
        </NetworkConnectionObj:Destination_Socket_Address>
        <NetworkConnectionObj:Layer7_Connections>
          <NetworkConnectionObj:HTTP_Session>
            <HTTPSessionObj:HTTP_Request_Response>
              <HTTPSessionObj:HTTP_Client_Request>
                <HTTPSessionObj:HTTP_Request_Line>
                  <HTTPSessionObj:HTTP_Method
datatype="string">GET</HTTPSessionObj:HTTP_Method>

<HTTPSessionObj:Version>HTTP/1.1</HTTPSessionObj:Version>
                </HTTPSessionObj:HTTP_Request_Line>
                <HTTPSessionObj:HTTP_Request_Header>
                  <HTTPSessionObj:Parsed_Header>

<HTTPSessionObj:Accept_Encoding>gzip</HTTPSessionObj:Accept_Encoding>

<HTTPSessionObj:Connection>close</HTTPSessionObj:Connection>
                  </HTTPSessionObj:Parsed_Header>
                </HTTPSessionObj:HTTP_Request_Header>
              </HTTPSessionObj:HTTP_Client_Request>
              <HTTPSessionObj:HTTP_Server_Response>
                <HTTPSessionObj:HTTP_Status_Line>

<HTTPSessionObj:Version>HTTP/1.1</HTTPSessionObj:Version>

<HTTPSessionObj:Status_Code>200</HTTPSessionObj:Status_Code>

<HTTPSessionObj:Reason_Phrase>OK</HTTPSessionObj:Reason_Phrase>
                </HTTPSessionObj:HTTP_Status_Line>
                <HTTPSessionObj:HTTP_Response_Header>
                  <HTTPSessionObj:Parsed_Header>
                    <HTTPSessionObj:Server>Apache</HTTPSessionObj:Server>
```

```
<HTTPSessionObj:Transfer_Encoding>chunked</HTTPSessionObj:Transfer_Encoding>
                  </HTTPSessionObj:Parsed_Header>
                </HTTPSessionObj:HTTP_Response_Header>
              </HTTPSessionObj:HTTP_Server_Response>
            </HTTPSessionObj:HTTP_Request_Response>
          </NetworkConnectionObj:HTTP_Session>
        </NetworkConnectionObj:Layer7_Connections>
      </cybox:Properties>
    </cybox:Object>
  </cybox:Observable>
</cybox:Observables>
```

definition includes information about the client server network communication outlining the layer 3 and 4 information. The definition also outlines layer 7 information including HTTP request and response information. The CybOX website, at the time of writing, includes a zip file containing more than two dozen samples to help users understand how to properly express cyber observables within the CybOX language.

The CybOX language, including information about how to join the community and access to the project repositories, is located on the following websites:

- CybOX website—http://cybox.mitre.org
- CybOX Community—http://cybox.mitre.org/community/
- CybOX GitHub Repository—https://github.com/CybOXProject/.

Commercial Offerings

One of the drawbacks to community-based sharing is the perceived lack of general availability of shared knowledge elements without belonging to a specific industry vertical or other gating factor to access the content feed. To overcome this hurdle, there are companies that either specialize in or have product offerings in the security or threat intelligence space. Commercial offerings are available in a variety of forms, as well as within a large range of price points. Enterprise can choose whether the goal is to supplement the community sharing access already available, or available to them via groups like NH-ISAC, as well as to decide that commercial offerings are the preferred way to digest new threat data for threat modeling. Regardless of the level at which an enterprise decides to subscribe, there are a few items to consider prior to using commercial offerings.

First, enterprises should determine how important industry-specific data is within their security intelligence to perform threat modeling. Depending on the size and type of organization, this may not be as critical. Think about the earlier example involving the Anthem breach,[1] industry-specific data played a very crucial role in determining the impact within the healthcare vertical. When evaluating commercial offerings, confirmation of data related to the specific industry vertical should be part of any or all of the thread feeds or services offered. This is not always the case. Second, how content is going to be processed via the commercial offering should be determined. Products and services offered at the time of writing range from raw packet captures (pcaps) to sample malicious code with an accompanied PDF outlining how the exploit or malware works "in-the-wild" (i.e., the malware's behavior or how the exploit is being used on the Internet). Some commercial offerings will be harder to integrate directly into an automated framework or integrate into other data being collected and shared via a community feed or multiple community feeds. A decision needs to be made as to whether the goal is to achieve a level of automation for faster decision making and alerting, thus requiring additional work to have certain commercial offerings benefit the enterprise, or if manual processes are acceptable. Finally, and following item two, some commercial products offer predefined "dashboards" or interfaces that will perform threat modeling as well as functionality similar to threat forecasting. Depending on the size of the enterprise, this type of service or solution may be the right fit based on resources within the company. Organizations choosing this type of product or service may not have a dedicated security group or large enough IT staff to build out the needed infrastructure to support digesting any feeds whether community driven or commercial. With a self-contained product, the enterprise can turn to a single source without needing to track the data itself.

In an attempt to remain unbiased and not indirectly promote specific commercial offerings or inadvertently omit a new offering, this book does not go into specifics about the services and products available at the time of writing. To find out more about companies in this space and the products and services they offer, major security conferences and events (including the exposition halls) can be leveraged as well as Google searches using keywords including "threat feed" or "security intelligence."

Staying Ahead of the Adversary

The threat landscape is continuing to grow and is ever-changing. Applications used in today's enterprises are becoming more complex with more and more lines of code needed to accomplish the tasks needed to keep organizations moving forward. Things become more complicated as organizations move services to the cloud and to application service providers making the enterprise border more transparent. This raises the bar for security teams and IT staff trying to protect enterprise assets from exploitation and company sensitive data from exfiltration. Furthermore, as the barrier of entry into the world of computer hacking and exploitation continues to thin, simple Internet searches return access to free exploit tools and organized crime syndicates willing to rent botnets by the hour.

The best way to stay ahead of the adversary is for the community to work together and alert each other to key indicators, or knowledge elements, as they are detected. This allows organizations around the world to alert each other to attacks, regardless of whether or not the attack is targeted to a specific industry vertical, allowing them to defend themselves as well as confirm if they have also been victim of the same attack. As previously outlined, this is possible when efforts are put into making this type of communication successful, as seen with the Anthem Breach[5] and the use of TAXII and STIX. As more enterprises and organizations work together through sharing threat intelligence, the efficacy will only continue to improve within the community sharing options. This will help all participants to minimize the total impact threat actors can have with the goal of minimizing the threat landscape and updating security solutions to mitigate the kill chain.

Summary

Enterprises are offered multiple options when looking into community-based sharing of knowledge elements for threat modeling as well as threat forecasting. At the time of writing, community-driven projects like TAXII and STIX, as well as the related projects like CybOX, are continuing to grow in popularity with more freely available options coming online. Enterprises should be not only consumers of these community-sharing options, but also producers of knowledge elements and share them within the same community feeds of which they are members. The advantages to sharing outweigh the disadvantages to joining these communities. Threat modeling with local data generated from the enterprise network provides just a small picture of what the total threat landscape represents. This will not give the enterprise a full view of what targeted threats may be "in-the-wild" and how they correspond to their threat landscape and kill chains. Threat modeling, combined with community sharing, provides the enterprise with the most holistic and near real-time view of the threat landscape allowing for better mitigation strategies as well as faster time to detection of security breaches. This also strengthens the enterprise's knowledge when performing threat forecasting.

6

DATA VISUALIZATION

Synopsis

This chapter covers the many ways to visualize your data for analysis and simulation. Not all data are to be seen from a two-dimensional aspect, sometimes it's easier to look from another perspective. Graphing and charting are often referred to as old and antiquated methods of data representation, changing how we look at data and how we can report on it.

Other ways of viewing the world of data means that we need to have a somewhat more flexible mind to except something new as a possibility for a different kind of representation.

Three-dimensional graphics are changing the way we see many things: everything from video games, to virtual office environments, to new security analytics. Looking down a virtual network pipe we are able to see the world of traffic flow and make connections to multiple hosts and subnets, making lateral pivots within the network and seeing data exfiltration in real time.

These are some of the things that we cover, please note that just because a technology was mentioned in this book doesn't mean that we endorse it or that we have purposefully excluded another technology.

Introduction

In this chapter we will cover not just the visualization of real-time data and the use of statistical key indicators, but we will also include the added benefits of flow data and the ingestion of data into large data analytics environments. Defining where the correlation and aggregation takes place helps us to find not just where the needle is in the haystack, but where the next needle may be found and, maybe, the purpose behind the next wave of attacks. Using large data analytics for finding new patterns we can slow

Threat Forecasting. http://dx.doi.org/10.1016/B978-0-12-800006-9.00006-9

the means of attack, which can aid in the quick discovery of other attacks based on the same behaviors.

Common Methods

Some of the most mainstream methods of visualization are the tried and true old-school graphs, charts, and scatter graphs. These are often clear indictors of the types of traffic coming through our networks, along with where they are coming from and how often.

More often than not many of these devices are just too old and antiquated. If the malicious actors aren't just using old methods of attack, why would we be using old methods of discovery visualization? In many cases the answer is an easy one: no budget and no time to implement based on the ever shrinking resource pool. Other reasons are the status quo in reporting, with nobody daring to ask about or looked into newer or better ways of representing data. This is due continuing stagnation of the workforce and a job market economy where members of the security staff are becoming complacent with a "if it's not broken why fix it!" attitude. The point is that it doesn't have to be broken to necessitate change. People for the most part hate change and can normally never see a reason for it.

Change is a necessity in the fluid intelligence community in which we live. Change is how we can ultimately make a difference by not just forecasting incoming threats, but also detecting larger patterns, getting an understanding of the precursory events that led up to the larger event of a breach and being able to take action against these in the future.

Other ways of visualization are dependent on large data analytics, which can be great for identifying many patterns and other useful events. However, unless the right question is asked and the relationship or correlation to other attributes has been made, the output can become useless, but we'll cover that later in this chapter. Representation and understanding of the data can mean the difference between identification of potential threats or breaches and not seeing them at all and being owned for many days, weeks, months, and sometimes years before finding out that your data now belongs to someone else.

Pivot tables incorporate data derived from the five tuple information gathered by multiple network resources: intrusion detection and preventions systems, firewalls, routers and switches, netflow collectors including Security Information and Event Management (SIEM) output. Pivot tables aren't just for spreadsheet users, as some databases are capable of making pivot tables and taking advantage of the correlation and sorting capabilities therein as seen below.

```
SELECT [non-pivoted column], -- optional
  [additional non-pivoted columns], -- optional
  [first pivoted column], [additional pivoted columns]
 FROM (
  SELECT query generating sql information for pivot
 AS Tuple Alias PIVOT (
  (Column for aggregation or measure column)
   -- MIN,MAX,SUM,etc FOR [] IN (
   1st column, to, last column)) AS alias ORDER BY clause
```

This allows for the quick representation of information as it can sort and perform aggregation of data and can also be used in defining of key indicators and attributes thereof. Pivot tables aren't just for business intelligence and analysts they are for everyone trying to get a better handle on things like unstructured data, data aggregation, key performance indicator optimization and statistical inference combined with data normalization. T-SQL (Transact-SQL) isn't for every application, nor is it for the mainstream analyst, it's just another way to look at large data sets and get useful information in a quick and meaningful way. The syntax for T-SQL isn't the easiest to learn but once you have mastered it, it gets easier; as does most things.

Once data are extracted it still needs to be manipulated in such a way that it makes sense to the analyst, a supervisor and in some cases an executive, who may be trying to understand why this is important to an organization and what to do about it. In many cases the person responsible for making the data presentable reverts to old representations where bar charts and line graphs are more prevalent, as these are also the most easily accessible data formats for shrinking budget costs.

Reporting capabilities play a large part in the visualization and representation of data. If you can't relate the information to the people who need to understand it, then you have failed in your ability to convey information. Understanding what it is you are trying to represent is the most important part of creating a report, along with its content, good or bad.

Being able to show and illustrate in many cases depending on who the report is intended for the who, what, why, where and when, can not only be the hardest challenge of the report but it can change the perception of the information based on not just it's accuracy but also its intent.

One of the most efficient ways to report creation is through the use of an automated approach: automatically updating based on dynamic data feeds with static variables. Based on an intelligence threat forecast, one of the most efficient and identified ways is a global map with key indicators on the map denoting events of interest. This allows the viewer to drill down into the indicator and look at an overview of the event—when the event happened (date and time); what the event was (a brief descriptor offering a more in-depth view); and information as to the source and destination of the event, including as much as possible to represent unstructured geographical information and network cost to determine where the source really is. Then there is the why. The why for an initial report can be, and in many cases is, more a case of "malicious actor exfiltrating data" and what that data may have contained than lateral movement in the network. There's quite a large range of what a malicious actor can do once a breach has happened, and in many cases is denoted as still under investigation.

Along with drill downs into key indicators there is nothing preventing the use of static graphs denoting the amount of access, protocol types used, events from a particular source and other aggregated data as it pertains to the event making it useful to the person ingesting the report and making actionable decisions

Big Data Analytics

Many people ask, why big data or large data analytics? They are just buzz words for fancy database schemas. Hadoop, Spark, Tez, and Redshift are just scalable databases with the ability to process large amounts of data across multiple nodes, enabling organizations and enterprises to uncover patterns in potential data breaches, correlate new information found because of these new patterns and see what else is out there. Patterns are more than just part of a breach, they are also part of a behavior. Behavioral analytics are also part of the pattern discovery. With enough data and other key attributes it's possible to begin discovering patterns in how a malicious actor performs certain tasks and by chaining those task together a full analysis can be done of when the attacker performs a lateral movement after a breach or how they perform reconnaissance on a target system. While many people claim to be unpredictable and random, most malicious actors stick to a set methodology 80% of the time. The other 20% is because a target may be more of a challenge or they stumble onto a system that is in the process of being compromised and simply tag along and create an additional beach head in the network.

What is a pattern? Normally it's any act that has been repeated at least three times by the same individual. Technically, it only need two acts to be repeated. While that specific filter of only two repeated acts may cast a larger net and possibly catch more noise, it's also more likely to catch more malicious actors, pivoting to the action for determination not just the number of times that it's been repeated. Various groups like to leave a note, others have a set game plan that they always adhere to, such as sending a warning and then performing a Distributed Denial of Service attack against the warned target. These behaviors while predictable are examples of behaviors that can be discovered by these types of large data analytics engines. Once discovered the parameters can be used to quickly identify these attacks with SIEM technology.

Understanding SQL and nonSQL databases are useful when dealing with large datasets. SQL uses structured tables, with well-defined data formats and records. NonSQL breaks the mold by storing data in documents that are grouped by collections of varying formats. Both are great to have as a complementary solution that allows for breakdown of the baseline information that can then be broken into larger data sets and correlated with more attributes that can be referenced.

Interactive Visualization

Virtual reality (VR) can be used to aid in the visualization of large data sets. One particular company (Deep Node) has found a way to make it work and quite successfully.

Fig. 6.1 is a way of showing packets using sphere's to depict network nodes, along with communication lines with attached network traffic payloads, that change the sphere's appearance

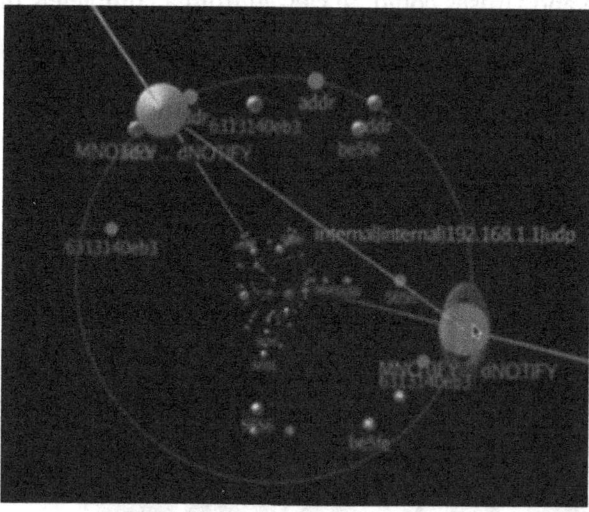

Fig. 6.1 Deep Node 3D view of data visualization.

to show an indicator of interest. In the representation above you can clearly see a user datagram protocol (UDP) packet being sent to a gateway address. This can be very useful when looking at large packet streams where there is a lot of noise, as this software is capable of identifying connections and applying packet capture filters to traffic of interest to the analyst by highlighting it in the pipe while other traffic flows around it. While this can make for a busy interface, it enables the analyst to view the entirety of the traffic stream and view other traffic that relates to other connections in and out of the network. Imagine being able to interact with a malicious users' lateral movement in real time. Taking action on a threat as it happens and shaping the outcome to something less heinous than a data breach.

This type of technology opens the doors for greater real-time action, where a SIEM will always be a SIEM, but data visualization can be so much more. Data reconstruction doesn't just end with packet capture replay. Packet capture replay is merely the tip of the iceberg in the bigger picture of analysis. With VR not only can you replay the event, but you can replay it visually and interact with that data on so many different levels, opening up a rich content world for drilling down into a database that was exfiltrated or seeing data flows and visual reconstruction of a stream while it's happening in real time. These are multidimensional file servers with access control offering a new level or dimension of the file system, offering new ways to view databases, data sets, and large intelligence feeds from an interactive streamed flow, and looking at potential examples of a breach, vulnerability, and exploit code. Malware and viruses could be viewed from a completely different perspective simply by lifting the veil that it hides behind and seeing what drops and call backs are made (Fig. 6.2).

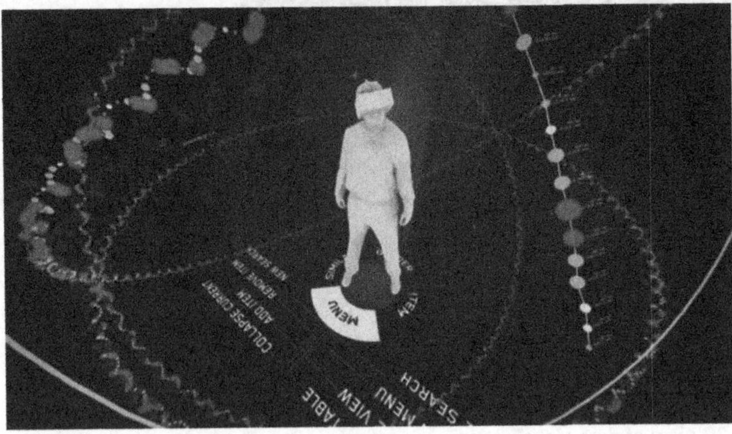

Fig. 6.2 3D representation of traffic from a different viewpoint.

Entire databases and data structures are mapped out with all the relationships and links pulled together in a drill down fashion with data representations being brought together in humanly readable formats.

Not Just For the Boardroom

It's been said that a picture is worth a thousand words, but a useful picture with an explanation of its data points can be priceless. Pretty pictures like bar charts, heat maps, infographs and the like are more than just a management tool that depicts nothing. They can be great ways to explain and relay important information and intelligence moving from target "A" to target "B."

Useful information that is both visually appealing as well as interactive is becoming the expectation within the industry. In the past what was more about extraction of information and parsing it into something readable and easy to digest has evolved into a user interface that is both useful and intuitive in design, while being able to relay a great wealth of information.

Geographical depiction of data has also become a commonality within various security operations centers, but it's also a meaningful way to disseminate intelligence as it impacts a region and industries. This covers in many ways a broad spectrum of events and information, but when looking at intelligence and understanding threat vectors, it can be extremely useful.

On the other side of this graphical depiction is the noise that it also often generates, as often it fails to include and associate the why with the who of the situation. Many groups are unknown to the victims. Having a good intelligence feed or report on what groups or organizations are out there, including the political or social agendas of said groups, can be a great way to provide insight as to their purpose or the message that they are trying to send to the industry.

Having knowledge of hacking groups' manifestos can help define the source of an attack, as each group has an overall code of ethics that they abide by. It's also known that every group has a bad egg here and there and ascension within the ranks is bound to happen. Knowing this isn't a definitive method of deduction, so much as it is useful when creating a means of determination. The attributes of methods of recon, attack, and exfiltration are to be noted. Not everyone has the same methods and some people within the groups often use the same methods time and time again. Behavioral analytics plays a big part of this.

The bigger picture can be seen as having a value, although others see it as a priceless artifact. Sadly, the nature of the image is that of a moving target. It's a fluid image that changes on a minute-by-minute basis. Value truly comes in the form of not just a snap shot in time, but a timeline of events and patterns over time.

Along with the bigger picture of data visualization comes a contextual understanding. An understanding that seems to get lost upon translation, as it often comes from within the trenches and in making its way to the boardroom the message has been dumbed down to the point where it loses all significant meaning and is dismissed quickly. Keeping contextual messaging in the appropriate state is just as important as the interpretation of the data that are depicted. These are best relayed as a presentation to the board or at least a brief statement of the facts with no interpretation, keeping in mind that time is of the essence when it comes to threat intelligence and forecasting.

Summary

Data, Data, Data! I cannot make bricks without clay!

We are now in an age where data visualization is playing a bigger part in the threat intelligence industry, looking at larger patterns and identifying potential threats and breaches within networks; all of which needs to be viewed in an intelligible manner. Making data useful is easy; making it understandable for the masses is something else entirely. This has become a reality for many security vendors, reporting data with no way for the analyst to see exactly what it is that is being carried forward by way of these large data streams. As mentioned in Chapter 9, being able to join the dots and make something meaningful and easy to digest not just at boardroom level but at all levels is part of the success behind many great visualization tools.

Visualization of a forecast in many occasions can be like that of a weather forecast. At times it can look like the beginning of the apocalypse and other times it's just a storm. Interpretation and the ability to review all the data points and visually recognize the storm from the apocalypse is the difference between a good analyst and a bad one. The doom and gloom of many visualizations will make things appear as if the sky is falling and what is often missing from this is the potential for a mitigation or solution to be put in place, to nullify or capture and observe the attack properly routing it to a black hole network where the traffic can be captured and replayed with network flow, and the event properly documented.

Keep in mind that when visualizing data, it is often good practice to look outside the accepted area of what is the commonly used reporting practice for your organization, as the problem might be in the relaying of the issue. Many organizations rely heavily on a set type of document or daily presentation format that contains many pretty pictures with very little context around it. So the content is discussed, but very little is understood. In a breach that I worked for a client, the employee was being complacent and posting sensitive company information on a public website for easy access to various notes, passwords to critical databases and methodologies so that he could move from work site to work site as a contractor. After a thorough investigation, the site had been indexed by many search engines, both foreign and domestic. The data were used by outsiders to take advantage of critical infrastructure, causing a mass password change, and a larger investigation of not just the data at rest, but what customer's records it was linked to, which were now at risk, in addition to everything that this person had touched from a development perspective. Visualizing this incident took some time to document and report on, but the forecast associated with the lost information taught us how we could now defend against the loss of information and how to prevent such a thing happening in the future.

7

DATA SIMULATION

Synopsis

In this chapter we cover several topics, such as understanding data simulation, what it is, how it is of great importance when dealing with Indicators of Interest (IOI) and Indicators of Compromise (IOC), and the difference between simulation and emulation. We will be covering simulation and the analytical engines that assist with the data inputs and simulations, and looking at the different types of simulation, along with some data sandboxing, and how the potential use of quantum tunneling can assist in the analytical side of the simulated traffic.

We will also cover how data simulation can be used in threat forecasting as a proactive tool to help and assist security teams remediate/mitigate threats within the enterprise, to avoid being breached due to a threat that is potentially harming many companies and agencies regionally, vertically and globally.

Introduction

When most people think of data simulation, they immediately start thinking about metallurgy, physics, DNA sequencing and evolution predictability. Simulation of data goes much further than that, and is on a larger scale than most would be willing to tackle. This chapter will cover using everything from low-end hardware to quantum super computers to perform data simulation. Many people believe that to do any kind of simulation you need hundreds of thousands of dollars and high performance computing clusters with extremely high bandwidth between them. The truth of the matter is that it's all relative. Relative to what is being simulated, over what period of time, and how fast you want to be able to complete your simulation. Simulations

Threat Forecasting. http://dx.doi.org/10.1016/B978-0-12-800006-9.00007-0

are used a forecast models and not just for weather forecasts. These models are the focal point of larger data analytics. They are important, as even though finding the needle in the haystack can be an easy task in a limited exposure breach, looking at all the data in an enterprise-wide breach becomes a daunting task without the use of larger analytical engines sifting through the data and, on a more proactive side of the fence, looking at the incoming traffic and the patterns to forecast when an attack is on the verge of happening.

Traffic Simulation vs Emulation

Traffic simulation is thought of in generation, replay or both. Although it is commonly referred to as event driven simulation or discrete-event driven simulation. Open source software exists for most popular platforms allowing the end user to simulate entire labs of equipment without the need to spend large amounts of the budget on equipment. The down side is that most of the time many of these environments don't allow for real time interactivity. Below is a short list of many of the open source variants that perform network simulations:

- NS2
- NS3
- OMNet++
- SSFNET
- J-Si.

The NS2 and NS3 products require you to script the initial lab environment using a Tcl script language with object-oriented extensions developed at MIT. From there the script is executed and event scheduler, network component and plumbing for the simulated network are setup and as the simulation executes it creates results that branch into analysis and open up a NAM Animator. A Nam is a Tcl/TK-based animation tool for viewing network simulation traces for further analytics, with the ability to provide visualization of the topology of the simulated network along with packet level information.

Network emulators, do just that. They allow you to build by giving you the ability to simply drag and drop network objects and link them together, providing the end-user with the ability to configure the link type and method of communication. Many of these emulated sandboxes are restricted by the hardware limitations of the physical host:

- IMUNES
- CORE
- Cloonix

- Marionnet
- Mininet
- Netkit
- VNX and VNUML.

All of the above-listed emulators give the end-user the ability to create networks safely in a non-routable, sandboxed environment, much like the simulators can, with the exception of real time interactivity. Some of the tools allow you to create simulated networks with independent physical workstations. This allows the end-user to host a very unique environment for testing real traffic against, while potentially simulating an entire enterprise grade network, with the only caveat that there must be enough processing and memory in multiple servers or workstations to accommodate the demands of the simulated environment.

These tools can help you create, generate and simulate network traffic in unique environments that allow for testing of threats. They allow you to create and tune for threat types need to be for the perfect storm, to some sort of diversionary tactic, to one that will only be posed in a particular environment, to something more generic that can make a larger impact on more targets.

When forecasting likely events based on patterns and simulations it's also just as important to have a good understanding of how the threat works, and what the impact of it is. Otherwise you are likely to end up with a bunch of people spreading fear, making the threat out to be more than it really is and only reporting it's spread without know why, to what end and what the deterministic nature of the threat is. Things to look out for in the wild are people spreading mythical news of viruses existing with no proof or sample code. Stating what the effects are and how it spreads, all in the name of gaining personal attention. On the flip side of this spread of misinformation are those who get spun about and get scared, and so the news travels from one blog to another and it soon becomes a story blown out of all proportion with no proof of its existence.

Environmental

Stochastic or forward modeling allows for the predictability of the model and parameters not just from the simulated patterns data, but also from data that have already been attained , adjusted and screened.

This normally involves the running of many generated simulations, often in the thousands of said generated simulated pattern, which are then summarized in a range of variations in the pattern. Using such things as scatter graphs as representations, the most likely outcome will be based on the data being consistent with few random variables. Hence, the importance of knowing how a threat works. It's infinitely easier to forecast once you have an understanding of what is vulnerable and whether the means of the threat is something that can be performed outside the enterprise or if it needs to come from within. Other more common methods of simulation are done using statistical modeling and differing algorithms consisting of Gaussian and spatio-temporal math.

Flow

From a forecasting methodology understanding the way information and bits travel throughout a network is an important part of making choices based on an external threat. Where does you network start and stop? Most networks start at the perimeter and finish at the end of the distro switches. Fifteen years ago that would have been a somewhat true statement. The problem is that there is increasing implementation of Bring Your Own Device (BYOD) policies for employees of companies that have created them due to the lack of IT budgets for new and emerging technologies, and companies are without a full understanding of what they are signing up for. Now the network boundary is made up of pockets employees wherever they happen to be. Sounds like an unbelievable statement, but where I have access to company email and resources, that is where the boundary stands.

Knowing your environment is the key to understanding the types of threats that can penetrate it along with those that will exploit it. Insider threat is one of the larger threats that many companies are faced with, as many people are just ignorant of the impact of their actions or believe that company policy doesn't apply to them as they know the difference between right and wrong.

In one case that I was involved in investigating, the developer was publishing all his work on a publically hosted web service in Utah. On the surface it doesn't sound like that big of a deal until you get a little closer in. The developer was working for an undisclosed federal agency at the time and was working on a very sensitive project that handled personally identifiable information and he thought that for ease of access it would be great if everything from admin level database credentials to web server passwords were to be stored on this publically hosted web site, in clear text with no form of authentication. The site had been indexed by every major search engine in the world and cached by several nations that aren't friendly with the government.

While many of the credentials stored in the public website are only accessible from the inside, getting inside this network later proved, several years later, to be easier than you could imagine.

The network boundary has become the illusion that some people feel is a definitive line in the sand stating that this is where it all starts and this is where it all stops. Everything is protected by a firewall that is mostly installed in name only, as many companies allow social media, share point collaboration, cooperate social media inside and outside of the supposed protected networks. This opens doors to many unwelcomed visitors.

Knowing the flow of your network becomes a task that no one person can keep up with. Even if multiple choke points that all traffic must pass through allows for greater inspection, it still adds up to a greater need for data visualization and analysis.

Data Sandboxes

The virtual play area for analyzing statistical, analytical, behavioral and object data using large data analytics is the bases for computing power and generating the results from multiple inputs and data sets. This is achieved using many of the analytic engines that are available today. A perfect example of a mature analytics engine is Hadoop and the use of Horton Works. Horton Works adds a nice graphical user interface (GUI) to an otherwise daunting user experience with multiple command lines where the user would need to be a somewhat expert user to get anywhere. Horton Works creates a simplified work flow for the user and allows the user to access the resources and create models and work with multiple datasets as needed. This also includes a large amount of systems to break down the heavy load of larger datasets and distribute the load accordingly.

It's not all fun and games in these sandbox environments, as many of these datasets are from actual data and these environments aren't cheap, in the traditional sense of using lots of bare metal hardware. Amazon Web Services allows you to create extremely complex and large scale Hadoop clusters quickly and without the overhead of a traditional datacenter. Large sandboxes have been used to analyze malware, viruses, trojans and other malicious actors in the wild.

Sandboxing malware has been around for many years dating back to the early 2000s with the analytics sandbox by Norman and quickly an entire industry around analytical and statistical sandboxes came to life. Analytical sandboxes had mostly been a commercial offering, but shortly thereafter many of the good ones became open source. Statistical sandboxes for the most have always been free in one way or another. You never find yourself paying for software directly, the cost comes in the form of the man hours and hardware that it takes to build and run the software. Many sandboxes demand a specific type of system such as Hadoop and Horton Works implementation so that the system can be implemented on a fairly stable and testing cluster base. After compiling, optimizing and testing a statistical sandbox, the first thing that needs to be kept in mind is the question. Using a statistical sandbox isn't like using an analytical sandbox where you insert the malware or data for analysis and see what pops out the other end. Statistical sandboxing requires some knowledge of the data going in to get the right answer on the other side. Many would argue that if you know what the answer is going to be then why do you need a computer and an investment of thousands of dollars in man hours building it? Because it's not that you don't know what the answer is, it's that you are searching for the parameters of the question or at least the statistical point of view from which you are going to answer the question. This process can take some trying to massage the data to proper representations without skewing the true results.

Data integrity is just as important as the integrity of the person that presents them. Using a statistical sandbox with the parameters set by the requestor aides the presenter, as the output data are representative of the input and the search parameters. Knowing the data types being input into the sandbox helps save time and effort when formulating the search parameters to gain the correct output. Labels and tags can be represented after the task has been performed that skew the data, as it's not a true representation of the output. Maintaining the original data tags and meta are key to the integrity of such output.

Analytic Engines

Simulation also requires a certain amount data gathering, some of that information is attained through large data sets and having it parsed through data analytics engines. Many instantly start thinking Hadoop and Berkeley Data Analytics Stack (BDAS). Yet there are many other solutions that get the job done quicker and in a more scalable fashion. MapReduce can now be done with tools like Spark, which now includes an interactive SQL as opposed to a non-SQL method. This allows people to migrate from other antiquated databases like mysql to Cassandra and then to Spark using the shark interactive sql tools, along with real-time analytics. This can then be integrated into machine-learning base

(ML-base) and the analytics output to a graph using other open source tools like GraphX.

Creating big/large data analytics applications can be done by cobbling together different systems, but the easiest way is to use engines built on top of the same platform. The ability to compete with overly optimized solutions gets harder with some applications, but adding a few more nodes to the cluster can make up for the short falls of un-targeted solutions, and this can be done with a little extra raw power. The performance of an integrated system will eventually become more convenient, as everything will perform as a single suite of tools instead of cutting from tool "a" to tool "b" and then into a visualization system.

While aging technology like Hadoop is being focused on commercialization, other open source software vendors are making greater in-roads with regards to innovative methods for solving the bigger picture, reducing costs and making big data more affordable.

Historical pattern recognition with real-time data capture and analysis can show you where and how to intervene before it's too late. Using multiple data sets and inputs from multiple sources can make for a great single picture.

Quantum Computing

In many ways quantum computing was considered a failure in the late 1990s due to a general lack of technological advancement and closed-minded scientists forever trying to push everything into a two-dimensional (2D) state. Now technology has advanced to the point and the realization that not everything needs to exist in a 2D world, but by using long-range mathematical equations, quantum tunneling has been deemed acceptable. Technically this is achieved by an API of sorts called a quantum machine instruction (QMI) by using a higher level application written in C, C++, Fortran or Python. Vendor tools for creating language translators and optimization problems are being used to directly program the system by using the quantum machine language to issue the QMI. The idea of quantum mechanics has been around for the past hundred or so years with very little in way of understanding or development until quite recently. Two scientists from the UK have recently been proving theories from the mid-1700s on quantum physics. These scientists have proven and correlated multiple researchers, who were on the edge of having a full understanding of quantum physics without looking at all the theory, math and possibility. Proving that quantum theories correlate with one another gave a company in Canada an idea for how to perform quantum math using the similar theories to those that the UK scientists have found and published.

The theory of using long-range math is that if the problem is left in the system for a day verses an hour the result of the day-long test will be more accurate and more concise than that of a complex problem loaded an hour before extracting the result. From an analytical stand point using quantum computing for analyzing malware and behavioral threats by itself is a colossal waste of time and money, as many threats are short- to near-term events that happen before its predictability can be finished. Long-term or slow aggressors, who are constantly trying to sneak by, looking inconspicuous amongst the rest of the noisy network traffic, would be easier to find if such a system could be augmented with a large data analytical engine automatically passing the quantum tunnel computer QMIs for larger pattern matching and events over time.

It is possible to interact with quantum tunneling at many levels, as stated above, and solving problems and performing analytics can speed up problem solving and exponentially shed light on an otherwise dark net that lurks in the shadows on the internet.

Summary

So the question is, how does all this information help to solve the big picture of threat forecasting and is this something the enterprise needs or can afford? The answer isn't going to be a simple one. Every enterprise network is somewhat unique in every way as are their markets and the types of threat that come knocking on the door. Most enterprises will have a legitimate need, but unfortunately the cost doesn't necessarily outweigh the return on the investment in the short term. After taking into account not just a reactionary benefit of using an analytical engine on existing data but using technology that can collect information from the wild and correlate it and add it to the simulation model, can a very proactive forecast be provided with a high degree of accuracy based on event timing, allowing security teams to take preventative measures?

Forecast models for threat forecasting are not something that you can just download off the internet and they will magically starting producing useful threat forecasts. It takes time and effort to work out a model that fits the enterprise. Generic models can get you so far, but it will not know anything about the network, what types of hosts are on it or how vulnerable it is. A good threat model can be generic as long as it is relevant to the enterprise.

When building a model think about what is in the network, how much of it is exposed to the world, is there a BYOD policy and what controls are around it, and how many host are running unsupported operating systems (and that is just the tip of the iceberg). Working with large sets as previously stated requires a lot of knowledge regarding the type of data, where it's coming from and what you want to do with it. Simulation of data isn't just about simulating data to get a specific outcome, its purpose is to simulate traffic that would be the root of the perfect storm in the enterprise, as many simulations don't take everyday traffic into account when looking at the bigger picture of vulnerability.

8

KILL CHAIN MODELING

Synopsis

This chapter covers the dissection of the kill chain model and the types of tools that can be implemented to assist with breach detection, analyzing data and sending it to larger analytical engines for further analysis. Many of the tools that we discuss in this chapter are just examples of what can be used and how they can help fill the gaps in security and strengthen the defenses against attacks.

Introduction

In this chapter we will cover various components of a kill chain, the uses for various technologies that assist in the detection and prevention of major breaches. Although we will keep in mind that the key to detection and prevention comes down to placement, we will go deeper as we go on. We will also cover many other options with regards to open source tools and their functionality. Please also note that the mentioning of these tools isn't an endorsement in any way, other examples are tools you can use to achieve some of the goals by not just looking at a dissection of the kill chain, but by filling some of the gaps in your existing infrastructure.

Key Components of Kill Chain Modeling

This can be broken down into several different components; keeping it as simple as possible is often the easiest way. The first component is planning, defining the target, being clear about the goal of the attack and making sure that if there is more than one attacker all team members are on the same page. A planned offensive often works best if there is a distraction followed by the malicious act in parallel. Making the distraction really big and noisy

Threat Forecasting. http://dx.doi.org/10.1016/B978-0-12-800006-9.00008-2

means that everyone pays attention to it first. When the noise dies away, the malicious act has already been executed. Not to say that we do this type of thing, it's more of an observed method seen in the wild. The second step is reconnaissance, which is closely linked to the planning stage and can cause a step back in planning based on what is gathered. Intelligence collection on the target is one of the most important steps, as this tends to dictate the method of the primary attack in many cases and along subsequent attacks yielding multiple options for performing malicious acts. Once all the planning is complete, meaning that the objectives of the operation are clear, any issues of overlap or task assignments, then steps one and two are complete and it is now time to move on to step three. This step tends to be fairly straightforward, as it's an execution of the carefully gathered intelligence and, depending on how carefully the intelligence was gathered, the target won't see the attack coming only that they are being attacked from multiple sides all at the same time. With the first wave being the most redundant and useless of attacks, making lots and lots of noise, and waking the night shift analysts. While the noise continues the real attack happens and the malicious actors compromise the network leaving with the information they first set out to get, setting up a beach head for easy access to get more information and returning to dig deeper.

After this the attackers own the enterprise, as many enterprises networks can take months to find that an attacker owns their network and has administrator/root privileges on all critical infrastructure.

A beach head normally consists of installing a command and control mechanism for ease of access from a remote node. Some of the better command and control software will randomly change ports and signal a control channel as to what port to use to access the system that has the command and control system on.

Detecting this in the kill chain can be accomplished in many ways. It's like manual labor, where having the right tool for the job makes easy work of the task. Many of these tools are found in tier one security appliances, allowing the security administrators to apply policies to malicious traffic sending them to a black hole network or honey net, which looks and feels like a great place to start digging for a juicy network that they then can't get out of.

Leveraging Big Data

Leveraging big data is addressed elsewhere in this book. Data in general is becoming richer in terms of content. Andrew Brust really does a great job in defining big data that captures the essence in his blog post on ZDNet.

"This blog is about an industry area that has come to be called 'Big Data.' The excitement around Big Data is huge; the mere fact that the term is capitalized implies a lot of respect. A number of technologies and terms get mentioned in the context of Big Data, with Hadoop chief among them, 'data scientist' often not far behind and sometimes NoSQL thrown in for good measure.

It's a bit unorthodox to start a blog post – especially a first post for a new blog – with a bunch of terms unaccompanied by definitions. But that's a perfect metaphor for Big Data itself because, frankly, it's not rigorously defined. Meanwhile the term is already entrenched – not just in the industry lexicon but in the mainstream vernacular as well.

What about Big Data is concrete and certain? We can safely say that Big Data is about the technologies and practice of handling data sets so large that conventional database management systems cannot handle them efficiently, and sometimes cannot handle them at all. Often these data sets are fast-streaming too, meaning practitioners don't have lots of time to analyze them in a slow, deliberate manner, because the data just keeps coming.

Sources for Big Data include financial markets, sensors in manufacturing or logistics environments, cell towers, or traffic cameras throughout a major metropolis. Another source is the Web, including Web server log data, social media material (tweets, status messages, likes, follows, etc.), e-commerce transactions and site crawling output, to list just a few examples.

Really, Big Data can come from anywhere, as long as it's disruptive to today's operational, transactional database systems. And while those systems will be able to handle larger data sets in the future, Big Data volumes will grow as well, so the disruptions will continue. The technologies used for creating and maintaining data, it turns out, are just not that well-suited to gathering data from a variety of systems, triaging it and consolidating it for precise analysis.

Perhaps you've heard of other terms, like Business Intelligence, Decision Support, Data Mining and Analytics, and wondered whether they're part of Big Data or technically distinct from it. While these fields may have started out as distinct endeavors, they are often folded in to the Big Data discussion. Sometimes when that happens, it may seem that people are merely conflating things. But it turns out that Big Data is still evolving, and as a term it's malleable. In a way, Big Data is a startup that's still working out its business model.

I've been working with database, data access and business intelligence technologies since the mid-1980s, so Big Data quickly became a logical interest for me. What's interesting, though, is that Big Data purists sometimes seem unaware of the data technologies that have come before, and miss out on the knowledge and experience those technologies represent. A few Big Data wheels have been re-invented ones" (http://www.zdnet.com/article/big-data-defining-its-definition/).

When it comes to applying Big Data principles to effective kill chain modeling and threat forecasting, it requires the use of large complex and unstructured data sets that need to be normalized quickly in order to get an effective result when applying the structured data against various applications such as threat forecasting and kill chain modeling. The kill chain model, as mentioned above, is fundamental to understanding the gaps and overlaps in the security controls that you have currently deployed or are considering deploying. The ability to model your internal security controls is critical in really understanding your exposure and there are many modeling tools that can provide that modeling and insight that will be discussed below.

Tools Available

There are many tools available for mining data, modeling data and viewing threat intelligence, such as Maltego, Splunk and Tenable. There are many more commercially available tools but these are a great start in terms of putting together large data sets and connecting the dots.

Obviously having more data points to work with increases not just the amount data collected but also the amount of analytics needed to distinguish the Indicators of Interest (IOI) and Indicators of Compromise (IOC) from the noise. Understanding the functions and expectations of these tools helps you keep a perspective of the types of data you extract from your analytics. Tenable for instance will be able to into not only provide great insight the vulnerability data for the configured subnets, but also assist with the overall Bring Your Own Device (BYOD) policy, by performing a constant discovery scan of the network and also reporting that information.

Splunk is a great log aggregation and analysis tool that competes with many security information and event management systems in the industry and can truly open the eyes of many security analysts. It has multiple dashboard applications, providing application management, and network flow information, and it can also be used to track event information on external network intelligence system, like cuckoo and cisco's botnet tracking security suite.

Maltego

The following is a snippet of the power that the use of Maltego can provide you with from their website. "With the continued growth of your organization, the people and hardware deployed to ensure that it remains in working order is essential, yet the threat picture of your 'environment' is not always clear or complete. In fact, most often it's not what we know that is harmful - it's what we don't know that causes the most damage. This being stated, how do you develop a clear profile of what the current deployment of your infrastructure resembles? What are the cutting edge tool platforms designed to offer the granularity essential to understand the complexity of your network, both physical and resource based?

Maltego is a unique platform developed to deliver a clear threat picture to the environment that an organization owns and operates. Maltego's unique advantage is to demonstrate the complexity and severity of single points of failure as well as trust relationships that exist currently within the scope of your infrastructure. The unique perspective that Maltego offers to both network and resource based entities is the aggregation of information posted all over the internet - whether it's the current configuration of a router poised on the edge of your network or the current whereabouts of your Vice President on his international visits, Maltego can locate, aggregate and visualize this information. Maltego offers the user with unprecedented information. Information is leverage. Information is power. Information is Maltego.

Maltego is a program that can be used to determine the relationships and real world links between:

- People
- Groups of people (social networks)
- Companies
- Organizations
- Web sites
- Internet infrastructure such as:
- Domains
- DNS names
- Netblocks
- IP addresses
- Phrases
- Affiliations
- Documents and files

These entities are linked using open source intelligence. Maltego is unique because it uses a powerful, flexible framework that makes customizing possible. As such, Maltego can be adapted to your own, unique requirements.

Maltego can be used for the information gathering phase of all security related work. It will save you time and will allow you to work more accurately and smarter. Maltego aids you in your thinking process by visually demonstrating interconnected links between searched items. Maltego provide you with a much more powerful search, giving you smarter results. If access to 'hidden' information determines your success, Maltego can help you discover it". (https://www.paterva.com/web6/products/maltego.php)

There are many important key takeaways that are mentioned above in relation to Maltego in terms of pulling together information and uncovering the unknown by visually and literally connecting the dots. The visual aspects of Maltego paint a picture that allows you to drill down to the information that is most important to you. In working with large data sets, you need to categorize and prioritize the data at the highest element with supporting data points that you can easily pivot, expose and correlate to other adjacent data points. The ability to perform these functions and move data around within a GUI allow an analyst to move quickly to the data sets that are important to him or her. The following is a screen shot of the Maltego user interface to provide more context as to the power of visual analytics (Fig. 8.1).

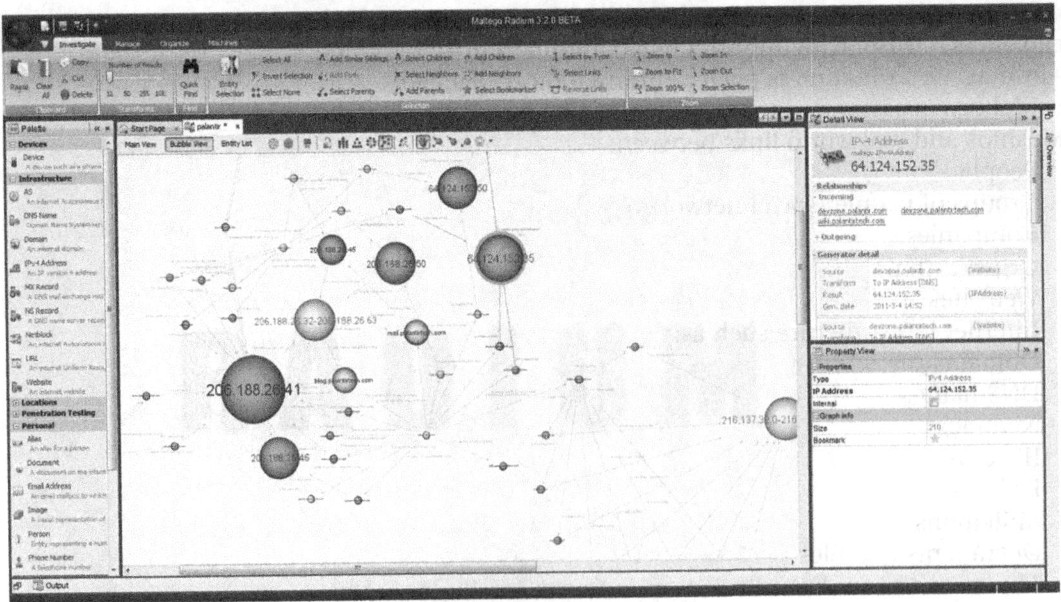

Fig. 8.1 Maltego user interface.

Each element that is rendered in the user interface allows the analyst to click and explore adjacent and relational data associated with each object. Similar techniques in automating big data within forecasting could be leveraged with a tool like Maltego in order to discover and track a threat from inception to detection.

Splunk

Splunk is another tool that can be used for kill chain modeling by conducting compromrise and breach assessment analysis. Splunk is like a swiss army knife in terms of all the ways in which you can mine data based on all the various data points that Splunk allows you to collect. Conducting a breach assessment based on multiple data points with Splunk helps you quickly pull together and connect the dots of said breach without written complex correlation rules. This is an important point because when you start discussing big data analytics the first thing that might come to mind is the complexity and the immediate need to hire a data scientist. The great thing about Splunk is that it takes the complexity out of the picture and provides a junior analyst with the ability to build relationships with ease. A common theme in some of these chapters is complexity of large data sets, but have no fear, there are a lot more commercially available tools that span beyond Maltego and Splunk that provide you with the ability to pull together large disparate data sets with ease.

Splunk isn't just for log aggregation either. It has multiple dashboards for managing and gauging the real time sales of an ecommerce site, dashboards for botnet tracking by various third party vendors.

Splunk also has integration applications into Amazon Web Services, Hadoop cluster health and welfare including end-to-end transaction monitoring. This extends into application management, IT Operations, Security and Compliance, Business Analytics and more.

Splunk also allows the user to create custom dashboards and representations of key data fields. When creating custom dashboards it's not a matter of creating a pretty picture for management, but creating a meaningful picture (this is discussed further in Chapter 6 – Data Visualization). Not all data can be represented with graphs, nor can it hold the same meaning. Representation of data needs to be exacting and clear. When someone looks at a security dashboard it needs to be clear about what it is and why it looks the way it does. Colors also play a big part in data representation; this is mentioned because the color red for instance, is generally equated to a negative result. Colors in general can mean different things to different people. Some people see a red number as a high alert, others think of it as purely a way of bringing a piece of information to everyone's attention. Colors tend to dictate whether people see data results as good vs bad. Where others merely see color as a means to express a differentiation between data types. Being able to modify and customize these types of reports is part of the success that Splunk has in creating custom reporting dashboards.

Something else to consider when creating a custom dashboard or application for Splunk is who it is intended for. Make it clear who needs to see what data and why it is important. Clearly document your logic around each representation and have a way of conveying the thought process involved in its creation.

OpenGraphiti

OpenGraphiti is unix-based tool that works great for multiple operating systems. This python-based tool allows you to graphically represent your network by mapping data flows allowing you to create custom datasets and drill down into a three-dimensional map without the need for or expense of oculus rift goggles. Viewing the multiple subnets can become visually overwhelming and many people tend to like looking at specific pieces, as it is easier to see the details and decipher what the map is attempting to show.

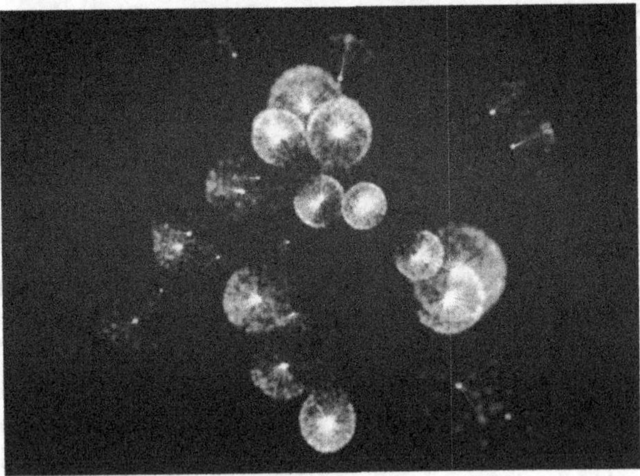

Fig. 8.2 Visualization with OpenGraphiti.

Two things need to be pointed out in Fig. 8.2. First is that the yellow dots are the nodes or systems on the network and the second that the pink bloom is a representation of an exploit kit. Many botnet trackers depend on this type of technology to track malware in the wild and as it allows the visually inclined analyst to see many problem areas within the environment without having to reformat the same data for other types of analysts with a very small learning curve. With some slight massaging of the data, the analyst is able to view large datasets quickly. This tool is currently being used to track CryptoLocker and CryptoDefense ransomware, Red October malware, and the Kelihos botnet; it is also being used in the various Syrian electronic army campaigns and carding sites.

The data visualization of this particular tool relies on a semantic network of relationships between multiple nodes connecting the dots in any relationship in data streams. From the highly complex to just a high-level representation, the analyst can create an immense amount of detail that he or she can show graphically based on the datasets that have been referenced. Please note that this is not entirely automatic and does require an understanding of how to build relational semantic networks.

"OpenGraphiti can apply the algorithms to affect the spatial representation and interconnectivity of the data nodes and edges" (Fig. 8.3).

Creation of Data Files

Suppose you have a graph

$$G=(V,E)$$

where V = {0, 1, 2, 3} and E = {(0, 1), (0, 2), (1, 2), (2, 3)}.

Suppose further that:

- Vertex 0 has the attributes:{"type":"A","id":0}
- Vertex 1 has the attributes:{"type":"B","id":1}
- Vertex 2 has the attributes:{"type":"C","id":2}
- Vertex 3 has the attributes:{"type":"D","id":3}

And that:

- Edge (0,1) has the attributes:{'src':0,'dst':1,'type':'belongs', 'id': 0}
- Edge (0,2) has the attributes:{'src':0,'dst':2,'type':'owns', 'id': 1}
- Edge (1,2) has the attributes:{'src':1,'dst':2,'type':'has', 'id': 1}
- Edge (2,3) has the attributes:{'src':2,'dst':3,'type':'owns', 'id': 1}

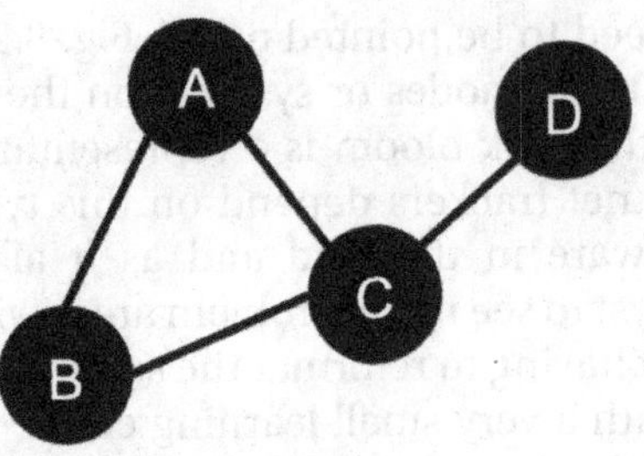

Fig. 8.3 Relationship modeling.

As you can see, there is a list of "node" objects, each of which contain the node attributes and IDs, as well as a list of edge objects, each of which have the edge attributes, and the fields src and dst, which indicate the source and destination vertices, respectively.

The following are few use case examples for OpenGraphiti include the analysis of security data, such as firewall, intrusion detection and prevention systems (IDS/IPS), and malware infection alerts could be visualized to expose a previously unrecognized patterns in a malicious actor activity, or even a misconfiguration of a technical control that allows too much, or too little, access to data, files, or networks.

Financial analysts could, for example, analyze data to track venture investment with data points such as the investor, the type of company being invested in (the target), its vertical market, or even the success (or failure) of the target before, during, or after the merger or acquisition. Trends may be observed to support a new model for investment and exit success above and beyond a simple spreadsheet.

Social network analysis (SNA) can be visualized to show relationships between people and their relationships with other people or things. Data could be visualized to articulate the interconnections across related networks in the fields of anthropology, biology, communication studies, economics, geography, history, information science, organizational studies, political science, social psychology, development studies, and sociolinguistics, among others". (Open Source Visualization with OpenGraphiti by Thibault Reuille and Andrew Hay)

OpenGraphiti is a great open source data visualization tool, but with large complex data sets it is important that you consider a platform that can leverage multiple graphics processing unit (GPU) for rendering the data quickly. Lastly, when it comes to data visualization and threat forecasting, OpenGraphiti provides you with the ability to customize and optimize the code to fit your specific needs.

STIX

STIX is covered in Chapters 4 and 5, but the following snippet from the STIX websites provides the detail on how STIX can be used in conjunction with kill chain modeling.

Kill Chains in STIX

Network intrusions can be seen as a series of actions taken in sequence, each relying on the success of the last. Stages of the intrusion progress linearly - starting with initial reconnaissance and ending in compromise of sensitive data. These concepts are useful in coordinating defensive measures and defining the behavior of malicious actors.

For instance, the behavior of a financially motivated intruder may appear similar to an espionage-motivated one until the final stage where they execute actions to steal their preferred type of information from the target.

This concept is often called a "kill chain" or a "cyber attack lifecycle".

Defining A Kill Chain

STIX represents kill chains using the KillChainType. Each kill chain contains a name, information about the definer, and a set of phases (represented using KillChainPhaseType. Phases can be unordered or follow each other using the ordinality attribute.

The example below defines a two-phase model from scratch. Additionally, Lockheed Martin published one of the first papers on kill chains and their own kill chain has become a de facto standard for this purpose. As such, STIX has defined static IDs to use for this phase. The example below also demonstrates how to create that kill chain definition using the existing static IDs.

Referencing A Kill Chain Phase

Kill chains are referenced by phase and kill chain ID from either indicators or TTPs using KillChainPhaseReferenceType. A kill chain reference in an indicator indicates that the indicator detects malicious behavior at that phase of the kill chain. A kill chain reference or definition in a TTP indicates that the TTP is used (malware, infrastructure, etc.) at that phase of the kill chain.

The example below demonstrates how to reference the kill chains (defined as explained above) on an indicator (Fig. 8.4). The indicator contents are empty to focus on the kill chain reference". (http://stixproject.github.io/documentation/idioms/kill-chain/)

```
<stix:Indicators>
    <stix:Indicator id="example:indicator-f33c2b75-aa60-4ffb-9829-3746ef233311" timestamp="2014-10-21T21:10:09.423000+00:00" xsi:type='indi
cator:IndicatorType'>
        <indicator:Kill_Chain_Phases>
            <stixCommon:Kill_Chain_Phase/>
            <stixCommon:Kill_Chain_Phase phase_id="stix:TTP-786ca8f9-2d9a-4213-b38e-399af4a2e5d6" kill_chain_id="stix:TTP-af3e707f-2fb9-49e
5-8c37-14026ca0a5ff"/>
        </indicator:Kill_Chain_Phases>
    </stix:Indicator>
</stix:Indicators>
<stix:TTPs>
    <stix:Kill_Chains>
        <stixCommon:Kill_Chain id="stix:TTP-af3e707f-2fb9-49e5-8c37-14026ca0a5ff" definer="LMCO" name="LM Cyber Kill Chain">
            <stixCommon:Kill_Chain_Phase ordinality="1" name="Reconnaissance" phase_id="stix:TTP-af1016d6-a744-4ed7-ac91-00fe2272185a"/>
            <stixCommon:Kill_Chain_Phase ordinality="2" name="Weaponization" phase_id="stix:TTP-445b4827-3cca-42bd-8421-f2e947133c16"/>
            <stixCommon:Kill_Chain_Phase ordinality="3" name="Delivery" phase_id="stix:TTP-79a0e041-9d5f-49bb-ada4-8322622b162d"/>
            <stixCommon:Kill_Chain_Phase ordinality="4" name="Exploitation" phase_id="stix:TTP-f706e4e7-53d8-44ef-967f-81535c9db7d0"/>
            <stixCommon:Kill_Chain_Phase ordinality="5" name="Installation" phase_id="stix:TTP-e1e4e3f7-be3b-4b39-b80a-a593cfd99a4f"/>
            <stixCommon:Kill_Chain_Phase ordinality="6" name="Command and Control" phase_id="stix:TTP-d6dc32b9-2538-4951-8733-3cb9ef1daae2"
/>
            <stixCommon:Kill_Chain_Phase ordinality="7" name="Actions on Objectives" phase_id="stix:TTP-786ca8f9-2d9a-4213-b38e-399af4a2e5d
6"/>
        </stixCommon:Kill_Chain>
        <stixCommon:Kill_Chain definer="Myself" name="Organization-specific Kill Chain">
            <stixCommon:Kill_Chain_Phase name="Infect Machine"/>
            <stixCommon:Kill_Chain_Phase name="Exfiltrate Data"/>
        </stixCommon:Kill_Chain>
    </stix:Kill_Chains>
</stix:TTPs>
```

Fig. 8.4 XML STIX kill chain scheme example.

Threat intelligence has and will continue to provide timely value in pushing real time threat intelligence to your organization. The ability to classify and categorize threat intelligence data via the kill chain provides you with information as to where in the process of the chain that said exploit has taken place. Data classification is important and it is important to understand just how far down the kill chain a threat has been classified. This really determines just how exposed you are to said threat. Within threat forecasting and additional set of key performance indicators (KPIs) would include: reconnaissance, weaponization, delivery, exploitation, installation and command and control. However, as mentioned previously in the book, the key with threat forecasting is determining the validity of a threat in a timely fashion. Unnamed threats will have to be generalized and at some point classified and categorized, which often has to take place after the discovery.

Summary

Implementing a well-planned and structured kill chain can be a difficult task fraught with budget restrictions along with architecture and design issues that may never get resolved, as the nature of many compromises becomes more and more complex. The key to such an implementation is to keep it as simple as possible with the least number of moving parts that can all move together in a smooth motion, so that integration can be capitalized upon with the least amount of silo'd appliances. Essentially everything has to work as a team. Complication will happen all by itself as plugging holes takes time and effort. There is always something you forget to think about.

There is no silver bullet out there that can do it all in a single appliance, the problem is that you would be putting all your eggs into a single basket, so to speak, and relying on a single vendor for every bug fix and up date. By spreading out over different vendors, you can increase the amount of threat intelligence and provide a greater depth of security when using multiple technologies.

9

CONNECTING THE DOTS

Synopsis

Connecting the dots is a symbolic way of stating we want to discuss all the topics within the preceding chapters by interweaving other related topics to show the value threat forecasting has for your organization. This chapter is broken into five main sections ranging from the comparing and contrasting of historical threat reporting and threat forecasting, to real-world examples where threat forecasting played a role or could have played a role in some of the major data breaches in recent time.

The first section discusses historical threat reporting and its relationship to threat forecasting. When discussing this topic with fellow colleagues in the information security industry, there was an automatic assumption that we no longer believe this is of any value. The opposite is in fact true. Historical threat reporting provides great value to organizations around the world, and these types of reports are available from security product vendors to security intelligence companies. There are several pitfalls associated with historical threat reports, however these are overcome when applying threat forecasting within your organization.

The next section dives into the state of the security industry by discussing the types of threats security products deal with as well as analyzing data from a third party, independent security testing lab. The types of threats security products need to deal with can be broken into three types. These are threats completely known to the security product, threats detected partially by the security product and threats completely unknown to the security product. The final type is where security products are the weakest and this is where threat intelligence combined with threat forecasting can help improve the gaps in your security coverage thus limiting exposure to your threat landscape. These unknown threats are best highlighted by the data within the study carried out by the

Threat Forecasting. http://dx.doi.org/10.1016/B978-0-12-800006-9.00009-4

cited independent testing lab, as they show, historically, that security products have had security efficacy issues.

Finally, we will outline how you can begin to apply threat forecasting techniques within your organization. We will give you a three-phased approach to entering threat forecasting to help lower the barrier to entry and make this new technique more accessible. Phase 1 focuses on research into threat intelligence feeds and improvements in your organization's existing security practices. Phase 2 introduces the creation of knowledge elements and helps you to begin threat modeling (and thus begin threat forecasting) using your data and, eventually, data from at least one threat intelligence feed. In the third and final phase you jump in with both feet and begin contributing to the threat intelligence community. Knowledge is power and by sharing knowledge elements you are enabling the global threat intelligence community through more actionable intelligence, as they are enabling your organization via your subscription to the feeds you are accessing. Successful implementation of threat forecasting techniques, powered by big data, will give you the data you need to better understand your organization's threat landscape and give you actionable intelligence so that your organization can help prevent the next major data breach.

This chapter is a call to action to begin applying the techniques within this book to improve your organization's security practices and procedures and begin threat forecasting.

Introduction

Before embarking on a journey into the world of threat forecasting, we want to bring the concepts discussed in the previous chapters together through several interrelated topics. First, we will discuss historical threat reporting and its value as well as its pitfalls. We will compare and contrast it with threat forecasting to show how these are actually complimentary and that historical threat reporting cannot replace threat forecasting within your organization. Next, we will discuss the state of the security industry by looking at the issues that exist for your infrastructure when applying traditional security protection using security products alone. Discussing the known knowns and unknown unknowns will show how threat forecasting extends your security coverage over more of the threat landscape. We will transition into a discussion about the tools available to assist with threat forecasting. There may be tools already within your organization that support, or have optional modules that support, threat forecasting. We will also discuss the use of open source software as community-driven software may provide better flexibility for your organization. Next, we will review some real-world examples of major data breaches and how threat forecasting could have played a role (or did play a role). Data breaches such as Anthem show how threat intelligence and threat forecasting can play a big role in protecting a community of organizations. Finally, we will outline how you can begin to applying threat forecasting techniques within your organization. We will give you a multi-phased approach so that adoption can be easy and successful.

Historical Threat Reporting

In general, we refer to historical threat reporting as the practice of summarizing events related to security threats, or particular focus areas such as mobile security threats, over a fixed period of time. Historical threat reports are generated by multiple types of companies and cover periods of time ranging from 3 months (or quarterly) to a year (or annually). Some historical threat reports change their focus topic each year, however the goal to provide a holistic view over a defined period of time, including any related trends and patterns, always remains the same. This style of reporting is the antithesis of threat forecasting. However, this does not mean it should be discredited or ignored, as valuable data can be extracted from it. Our goal is to outline the values and issues with this type of reporting, show how to leverage its value, and compare and contrast it to threat forecasting.

Value vs. Issues

Historical threat reporting, though noted as the antithesis of threat forecasting, provides value and we believe it is an important source of data for you and your organization. The first, and probably the most important, item provided by historical threat reports is an analysis of large datasets. The data points within these datasets today usually do not make it into threat intelligence feeds (please refer to Chapter 5 – Knowledge Sharing and Community Support) and the components that do are not fully consumable in a way that is useful. Vendor-based historical threat reports can discuss what their security intelligence teams have researched during the year based on what their customers have seen. These data can be valuable to review, as they are a summation of a large dataset that may not be consumable as part of threat intelligence feeds by one organization. Next, in relation to the first point, historical threat reports can be focused on discussing data breaches and correlating data across them. This can be extremely helpful, as sometimes these reports will focus on specific verticals that may relate to your industry's vertical. These datasets are unique and, like in the first point, sometimes do not make it into threat intelligence feeds. Finally, historical threat reporting can be compared to data being collected within your organization. It may help with highlighting areas within your security policies and procedures that need to be improved or may help with improving existing policies by reinforcing the efficacy of existing procedures.

Historical threat reporting is not without its flaws (or inherent issues). The first is due to the very nature of historical threat reporting. Historical reporting only focuses on what has happened in the past, thus giving you 20/20 vision on these events alone. Examining trends from a previous quarter or year does provide some insight into what the current trends in attack patterns may be, however these reports are not readily available for some time after the period they cover. This leaves a gap in the knowledge of the threat landscape that spans from the end of the historical threat report data up until the day it is published, which in some annual threat reports can be a void in threat intelligence of up to 4-months. The second issue is the static nature of historical threat reporting. Most historical threat reports are available as a PDF or infographic. This data cannot be processed automatically and leveraged by threat intelligence tools immediately upon publishing. There are some exceptions, like the Verizon Data Breach Investigations Report, where indicators are published via the VERIS threat intelligence community (please refer to Chapter 5 – Knowledge Sharing and Community Support). Finally, some historical threat reports include predictions about future events. Though grounded in (usually big) data, the data can be stale by the time it is analyzed. Furthermore, this data do not represent what is happening today or within your organization's specific vertical. One of the biggest flaws of historical threat reporting is the time that elapses between data collection and data analysis. Because of the time that elapses before historical threat reports are released, there are gaps in the threat landscape and any predictions made are already stale.

Leveraging Historical Threat Reporting

Even with the above outlined flaws, there is value within the historical threat reports generated within the information security industry. These threat reports are presented in different forms including pure infographics and are produced by different types of organizations from incident response to global threat intelligence. There is a wide range of reports to choose from and you only need to do a simple Google search for "annual network security report" to be given options to choose from. The following is a list of popular historical threat reports. It is not meant to be exhaustive nor does inclusion in this list equal endorsement by us:

- Verizon Data Breach Investigations Report[1]
- Cisco Annual Security Report[2]
- IBM X-Force Threat Intelligence Quarterly[3]
- McAfee Global Threats Report[4]
- Symantec Internet Security Threat Report[5].

All of these reports, as well as their counterparts, contain valuable information about the state of the threat landscape for the time period covered. This information can be valuable when performing threat modeling where data points being discussed overlap with potential attack vectors that may exist within your organization. Also, these reports may contain predictions of future security threats based on the trends discovered. These trends, though not a replacement for predictive analysis, may provide additional guidance on identifying critical areas within your organization's threat landscape.

Historical Threat Reporting vs. Threat Forecasting

Unlike historical threat reporting, the goal of threat forecasting is to combine real-world threat intelligence with data collected from within your organization to identify patterns or trends that are "in-the-wild", or out on the Internet, that may impact your organization. Threat forecasting requires you to take an active role in the threat intelligence community for it to be truly successful. This may require you to step out of your comfort zone. This is different from historical threat reporting where the data is provided to you, the consumer, via a static report which may contain antiquated data. Historical threat reporting may help

[1]Verizon Data Breach Investigations Report, Verizon, online, http://www.verizonenterprise.com/DBIR/.

[2]Cisco Annual Security Reports, Cisco, online, http://www.cisco.com/c/en/us/products/security/annual_security_report.html.

[3]IBM X-Force Exchange, IBM, online, http://www-03.ibm.com/security/xforce/.

[4]McAfee Labs, McAfee, online, http://www.mcafee.com/us/mcafee-labs.aspx.

[5]Security Response Publications, Symantec, online, http://www.symantec.com/security_response/publications/threatreport.jsp.

youfind a data breach that has already occurred, as it may discuss the details of other data breaches with similar threat landscapes to your organization. However, one of the goals of threat forecasting is to help prevent the data breach before it happens by examining current data to identify high-risk elements that need to be protected.

Table 9.1 is a quick reference for comparing historical threat reporting to threat forecasting. This table is not meant to be a complete comparison. We have outlined four key points about each to remember to help keep them separated and highlighted the goals each provides.

Table 9.1 Historical Threat Reporting vs. Threat Forecasting

Historical Threat Reporting	Threat Forecasting
• Overview of what happened within the period of time the report covers	• Leverages your data for better accuracy to your organization
• Sometimes provides predictions based on the upcoming year based on previous year trends	• Leverages third party intelligence to provide a holistic view of the entire threat landscape
• Static report generated on a fixed schedule (usually once a year)	• Shows what is happening today in the real world (even within your industry vertical)
• No ongoing updates about how your organization maps to the threats occurring "in-the-wild"	• Can help you improve your security posture prior to an attack or a data breach

State of the Security Industry

At any given time, someone within the information security industry can make a statement about the efficacy of security products (or the lack thereof) that may sound authoritative. These types of statements are made by security vendors about their security coverage protection versus the competition, by analysts working for research firms, by writers working for traditional or social media outlets and by testers working for security labs. The statements made by these sources need to be weighed accordingly depending on the motivations for said statements. For example, a testing lab may produce a report showing vendor X has the highest security efficacy within a given technology space; however, upon closer evaluation of the report, it is noted that vendor X sponsored the testing that this lab performed.

Please note that not all testing lab reports or vendor generated data should be treated as speculative. We, at a given point in our careers, have worked for either independent security testing labs or security product vendors (and we may be now, depending on when you are reading this) and have made such statements about the state of the security industry or about the efficacy of security products. The purpose behind this section of the chapter is to help lay the foundation for an understanding of what products are used today, the issues that are inherent within each technology, and clarify what security solutions are designed to detect. With this knowledge, an organization can build up their defenses and apply knowledge elements to defend against attack vectors not yet known using the security products they have deployed to protect their organizations.

Security Products Deployed Today

Organizations, whether enterprises or service providers, have a wealth of choices when selecting the security products to deploy within their networks. This section discusses some of the popular security products deployed today, including their strengths and weaknesses. However, this is not in any way meant to be an all-inclusive list. We strongly believe that defense in depth, or deploying a multi-tiered environment including multiple security product vendors, is the correct way forward for any organization. While it may be more convenient to have a single appliance solution from a deployment standpoint, a single point of failure is created within the infrastructure. Furthermore, we recommend a blended security vendor environment within your infrastructure. Deploying a single vendor environment, even if there are multiple products from that security vendor, only allows you to benefit from one research team. Deploying a blended vendor environment gives you access to multiple research teams who may have access to different attack vectors (i.e., different research data) giving better security coverage.

Next Generation Firewalls

A next generation firewall (NGFW) is today's iteration of a network firewall where the "N" could really stand for "now" instead of "next". NGFWs offer basic packet filtering or proxy-based decision making within layers 3 and 4 of the OSI model available within traditional, stateful, firewalls, however they expand their protection "up the stack" by also making decisions at the application layer (i.e., layer 7). Common features within NGFWs include application identification (and control), user-based authentication, malware protection, exploit protection, content filtering (including URL filtering) and location-based access control.

Traditionally, these security products rely on signatures for detecting attacks and malware, as well as some heuristics for detecting malicious activity and defining security coverage where signature may fall short.

For more information on the Open Systems Interconnect (OSI) model, please refer to the Microsoft knowledgebase article *The OSI Model's Seven Layers Defined and Functions Explained* located on their support website.[6]

Intrusion Prevention Systems

An intrusion prevention system (IPS) is a network security device that usually communicates with the network it is protecting at layer 2, thus it is usually "transparent" on the network. Most IPS solutions are designed to detect attacks targeting known vulnerabilities (as well as prevent them when configured to do so). Additional features exist within IPS solutions including real-time blacklisting (RBL), malware detection (and prevention) and application identification (and control). A newer generation of IPS solutions exist known as next generation IPS, or NGIPS, that include additional features to make them very similar to NGFWs. These solutions may be the right solution for organizations that have deployed a traditional firewall and are not looking to replace it, but want the "next generation" features/protection options offered by NGIPS and NGFW solutions.

Both IPS and NGIPS solutions are primarily signature based but they also use behavior detection for attacks that do not cleanly fit into a signature definition or if behavior is the best way to detect them (such as DDoS attacks).

Web Application Firewalls

A web application firewall (WAF) is a network security device or web server plugin built to protect web services running over HTTP (usually TCP port 80) and HTTPS (usually TCP port 443). WAFs primarily focus on layer 7 security (refer to the earlier discussion on the OSI model) with the goal of securing web transactions and blocking malicious transaction attempts and

[6]The OSI Model's Seven Layers Defined and Functions Explained, Microsoft, Online, https://support.microsoft.com/en-us/kb/103884.

man-in-the-middle attacks[7] including SSL downgrade attacks. Examples of malicious web transactions include cross-site scripting (XSS), cross-site request forgery (CSRF) and SQL injection. More advanced WAFs offer session integrity checks where they can add additional items to server responses, including keys like a cryptographic nonce, that clients would need to include in their requests. WAFs can also be purpose built solutions focused on protecting XML communications for web services that expose an XML interface following a standard such as Web Services Description Language (WSDL)[8] or offer a REST API. These solutions are commonly referred to as an XML firewall and can be integrated into WAFs as an additional offering.

Commonly deployed WAFs are usually reverse web proxies so that they can terminate SSL sessions allowing for full web transaction inspection. This also allows the WAF to have better control over server responses and manipulate them, as needed, prior to sending them to the requestor.

Endpoint Security

An endpoint security (EPS) solution is unlike the previous solutions discussed. Its sole purpose is to defend the endpoint (i.e., user desktop or laptop, data center server) and is usually centrally managed allowing the administrator to roll out global policies and perform scans on an endpoint as well as many other administrative tasks. EPS solutions are usually comprised of several common components including anti-virus protection, host IPS and application control. Traditional anti-virus protection is operated on an on-access (i.e., when a file was accessed by the operating system) or on-demand (i.e., when the scanner is told to perform an action) system, however EPS solutions usually include more advanced anti-malware protection extending into malicious URL detection and malicious network activity (such as command-and-control communications). Also, host IPS functionality is a subset of traditional IPS functionality providing coverage for vulnerabilities that are relevant to the endpoint including attacks targeting web browsers. Note that some host IPS functionality, depending on the security product vendor, may only operate in an intrusion detection (IDS)/alert mode and not actually block attacks targeting vulnerabilities or other malicious activities. Finally, some EPS solutions offer a

[7] Man-In-The-Middle Attack, OWASP, online, https://www.owasp.org/index.php/Man-in-the-middle_attack.

[8] Web Services Description Language (WSDL) Version 2.0 Part 1: Core Language, W3C, Online, https://www.w3.org/TR/wsdl20/.

level of application control allowing the administrator to limit access to categories of websites or specific websites based on a global policy.

The base functionality of EPS solutions is signature based detection with some solutions employing behavior analytics for detection of more advanced attacks. This allows research teams supporting EPS solutions to quickly roll out protection for known attack patterns.

Advanced Threat Detection

Advanced threat detection (ATD) solutions go by several different names, including advanced threat protection, however the goal is always the same. ATD solutions are designed to detect (and prevent in some cases) zero-day attacks and malware by using a combination of detection techniques. These solutions may be comprised of more than one product to provide the comprehensive security coverage the product vendor is looking to supply. This may include a dedicated sandbox/detonation chamber for executing malicious files and accessing malicious URLs as well as dedicated appliances for taking action based on the data provided from both the product vendor's research team and the results of analysis from the sandbox/detonation chamber.

ATD solutions use a combination of behavior analysis and signature detection, depending on which component of the ATD solution is being discussed. Sandbox/detonation chambers primarily use behavior analysis and look for changes within the environment being monitored. Dedicated protection devices may still use a level of behavior analysis; however, they will also use signature detection to aide in quicker detection thus leading to real-time protection/mitigation of attacks and malware.

Product Effectiveness Issues

The majority of security product vendors strive to provide protection from security threats. However, this can be a challenge for security vendors and their research teams, as the ever evolving threat landscape can change faster than these teams may be able to keep up with. Furthermore, attacks and malware can come in multiple variants, or replicates, adding to the complexity of the security coverage protection required. Polymorphic malware and exploit variants add to the depth of coverage needed to detect and prevent known security threats. To help validate the security efficacy of a security product, enterprises can look at third-party testing results to help confirm what products generally perform the best. As mentioned earlier in this section, third-party testing is offered in many different forms, including, sometimes, sponsored tests with a focus on market positioning and not on true efficacy. As such, the source of the data must be truly independent and vendor neutral to give the most accurate results.

An example of an independent, third-party, vendor-neutral testing is ICSA Labs. ICSA Labs, an independent division of Verizon, was founded in 1989 with a focus on third-party product assurance for end-users and enterprises. In cooperation with the Verizon RISK Team[9], ICSA Labs released a whitepaper, titled *ICSA Labs Product Assurance Report*[10], which outlined the first 20 years of independent security testing (performed by ICSA Labs) of products submitted for testing. This report contains some interesting data points with respect to how security products perform when put against publicly vetted test criteria. The first data we are going to review we will refer to as initial certification rate. According to the ICSA Labs report[2], it takes an average of two to four testing cycles for a security product to pass for the first time. Also, the initial pass rate is only 4%. Viewed in the inverse, the findings (or initial pass rates) show that 96% of products fail to meet the testing requirements. Finally, even with the additional testing cycles, not every product will meet the testing requirements. This rate varies depending on the technology; however, the overall average is 82% of products achieve certification from ICSA Labs. Table 9.2 outlines results from the complete report.

Table 9.2 Initial Certification Rate

	All Testing Certifications	Anti-Virus	Network Firewall	Web Application Firewall	Network IPS
First Attempt Pass Rate	4%	27%	2%	0%	0%
Certification Attainment Rate	82%	92%	86%	100%	29%
Testing Cycles Required for Initial Certification	Approximately two to four testing cycles				

[9]Verizon RISK Labs, http://www.verizonenterprise.com/products/security/incident-management-ediscovery/risk-labs.xml.
[10]ICSA Labs Product Assurance Report, ICSA Labs, Verizon RISK Team, Online, https://www.icsalabs.com/whitepaper/report.

Furthermore, products are continuously deployed within the ICSA Labs testing networks so that new releases and updates can be tested for conformance with the certification criteria that the product had previously passed. Also, as the testing requirements evolve, products are subjected to spot-checks, to confirm they are in compliance with any updates to the test criteria. Table 9.3 outlines the results seen over the 20-year period covered in the *ICSA Labs Product Assurance Report.*

Table 9.3 Retest Success Rate

	All Testing Certifications	Anti-Virus	Network Firewall	Web Application Firewall	Network IPS
Products that have criteria failures on retest	36%	30%	18%	50%	93%
Products that maintain certification	87%	87%	97%	80%	57%

Almost 40% of products that are retested, whether due to a software update or some other retest event, fail their retest. The percentage of failure increases as the complexity of the technology increases. This is best highlighted by the Network IPS retest failure rate of 93%. Also, the products that maintain certification also comprise interesting data. Though the overall percentage was high across all testing certifications offered by ICSA Labs (i.e., 87%), the more complex the technology the lower the percentage. Again, the Network IPS recertification rate was only 57% at the time of this report.

It should be noted that all ICSA Labs test criteria along with all product testing reports are available for free on the ICSA Labs website.[11] Also, all testing requirements, known as testing criteria on their website, are developed using a consortium model including industry experts, product vendors and enterprises.

The Known vs. The Unknown

Security coverage and efficacy of security products boils down to protecting against known attack vectors and, depending on the technology, the ability to detect malicious behavior.

[11] ICSA Labs website, https://www.icsalabs.com/.

This relies on research teams within respective vendors being able to identify, classify and express attacks (i.e., exploits targeting vulnerabilities),malware and malicious behavior in a way that their security solution can use to protect a given network. However, this becomes a game of the known versus the unknown. During his time as Secretary of Defense, Donald Rumsfeld stated the following during a 2002 Department of Defense News Briefing:[12]

> *"Reports that say that something hasn't happened are always interesting to me, because as we know, there are known knowns; there are things we know we know. We also know there are known unknowns; that is to say we know there are some things we do not know. But there are also unknown unknowns – the ones we don't know we don't know. And if one looks throughout the history of our country and other free countries, it is the latter category that tend to be the difficult ones."*

Although not his intent, former Secretary Rumsfeld outlines the root issue for security products. Security products can do (and usually do) a very good job at detecting and preventing, when configured to do so, known attacks and malware. Known attacks and malware are the known knowns for security products. Malicious activities and behavioral patterns fall into the known unknowns as security products do not know, necessarily, what is the cause of the malicious activity; however, they do know that something bad is occurring. In both cases, known knowns and known unknowns, most security product vendors will tell you that they perform well (and they probably do). This was highlighted earlier within the *Product Effectiveness* section of this chapter. Security products can do well, however some do struggle, with the items that fall into these first two categories (known knowns and known unknowns). The larger challenge for security vendors and their products are the unknown unknowns. As stated within the quote, these are "the ones we don't know we don't know".

As stated, this is the root issue for security products as, without any sort of prior knowledge, it would be hard to detect something you have no clue even exists. However, with the power of shared threat intelligence and applying the threat forecasting techniques outlined through earlier chapters, it is possible to empower today's security products to become aware of new threats before signature and heuristic updates are made available. Most security vendors provide the ability to apply custom

[12]DoD News Briefing (12 February 2002), Secretary Rumsfeld, D., General Myers, R., Online, http://archive.defense.gov/Transcripts/Transcript.aspx?TranscriptID=2636.

signatures or detection policies within their products. By collecting data provided via community threat intelligence feeds, these types of custom detection policies can be created and thus unknown unknowns, from the perspective of the security product, can be blocked until an update is provided by the security vendor's research team containing their specified protection. This new "power" can protect an organization from a new threat within their industry vertical as it impacts others. This is fully apparent when examining the Anthem breach as the key knowledge elements were published to all members of the National Healthcare Information Sharing and Analysis Center (NH-ISAC) allowing everyone within that industry vertical (members of the NH-ISAC) to determine if they had also been breached and also to set up protection in case the attackers used the same attack vectors against one of them. The Anthem breach is discussed briefly in Chapter 5 (Knowledge Sharing and Community Support) as well as in more detail in the Real World Examples section of this chapter.

Leveraging New and Existing Tools

To succeed at threat forecasting you need to select tools that will enable you to get the most out of the knowledge elements you create as well as knowledge elements you receive via threat intelligence feeds. You could be using tools within your enterprise today that may include components needed for receiving threat intelligence feeds and creating knowledge elements. The following sections discuss open source solutions and commercial offerings and how you could leverage them for threat forecasting and predictive analysis.

Open Source Solutions

Community driven tools, including open source solutions, can be the right choice for you and your organization. Open source solutions usually provide flexibility and extensibility beyond what commercial solutions offer. Some open source solutions do come with a higher barrier to adoption, requiring implementers to have a more solid grasp on items such as development languages and basic command line skills. This is improving within the open source community and with this also comes better documentation, user communities and other support-like tools that help lower the barrier of adoption and make open source solutions more accessible to the general IT community. Depending on the open source licensing model, organizations can modify the base version of the open source project to meet their needs while making proprietary extensions needed to work within their environment. Furthermore, the licensing may have the clause that changes need to be "committed", or submitted back to, the community. This supports growth of the open source tool including new features and defect fixing. The following is a list of open source solutions available today. Please note that being included on this list does not equal an endorsement from us:

- The MANTIS (Model-based Analysis of Threat Intelligence Sources) Framework[13]
- SPLICE add-on for Splunk.[14]

To find more open source solutions for your organization, Google search for "open source threat intelligence tools". We believe in supporting the open source community and using open source solutions when applicable.

Commercial Offerings

Sometimes open source tools require more investment of time and may require a skillset outside your comfort zone to deploy, configure and maintain. In cases like these, commercial offerings may be the right fit for you and your organization. Commercial offerings can bring an ease of use, knowledgeable support teams and other advantages over open source solutions that can help your organization when it already feels shorthanded. These solutions range from standalone offerings to modules of existing products you may be using already. This lowers, or potentially eliminates, any barriers to adoption getting you and your organization threat forecasting quicker. The following is a list of commercial offerings available today. Please note that being included on this list does not equal an endorsement from us:

- iSIGHT Partners ThreatScape
- LogRhythm
- Lockheed Martin Palisade
- Splunk Enterprise Security
- ThreatConnect
- ThreatQuotient
- ThreatStream.

[13]MANTIS Framework, Siemens, online, http://django-mantis.readthedocs.org/en/latest/.

[14]SA-SPLICE, Cedric Le Roux, Splunk Security Practice, online, https://splunkbase.splunk.com/app/2637/.

As previously mentioned, this list is not exhaustive and more tools are becoming available as threat intelligence becomes part of everyday life for organizations. More commercial offerings, as well as open source offerings, are available for review by performing a Google search for "threat intelligence platforms" or "threat intelligence tools".

Real World Examples

To best understand how the concepts discussed so far within this book come together, we will review some data breaches that occurred around the time of this writing. These examples cover everything from successful implementation of the topics within this book to lessons learned post data breach.

Anthem Breach Revisited

As at the time of writing Anthem Inc. (Anthem) is one of the largest insurance companies within the United States serving over sixty nine million customers or one in nine Americans.[15] The data breach was initially discovered on January 29, 2015, however the initial cyber security attack (thus creating the data breach) was believed to have occurred over a few weeks' period in early December 2014.[16] Anthem released an official statement regarding the data breach and in it outlined the involvement of the United States Federal Bureau of Investigations (FBI) and that Mandiant, known for their incident response team, had been put on retainer to assist with the data breach and subsequent hardening of their information security systems.[17] Organizations like Anthem have insurance policies, sometimes referred to as cyber risk insurance, to cover them in situations like this one. However, due to the large size of this data breach, the costs to Anthem were expected to exceed the $100 million policy they had in place with the American International Group at the time of the data breach.[18] The following is a list of items identified to

[15]About Anthem, Inc., Anthem, online, http://www.antheminc.com/AboutAnthemInc/index.htm.

[16]How to Access & Sign Up For Identity Theft Repair & Credit Monitoring Services, Anthem, Inc., Online, https://www.anthemfacts.com/.

[17]Data Breach at Health Insurer Anthem Could Impact Millions, B. Krebs, Online, http://krebsonsecurity.com/2015/02/data-breach-at-health-insurer-anthem-could-impact-millions/.

[18]Anthem data breach cost likely to smash $100 million barrier, C. Osborne, ZDNet, Online, http://www.zdnet.com/article/anthem-data-breach-cost-likely-to-smash-100-million-barrier/.

be included within dataset accessed and potentially stolen during the data breach:

- Names
- Dates of birth
- Social Security numbers
- Health care ID numbers
- Home addresses
- Email addresses
- Work information like income data.

Reviewing the Anthem data breach as just a data breach does have its value and organizations can glean some lessons from it. However, we have included it in this chapter not as a data point on data breaches and how bad they are (as we all can jump to that conclusion without a heavy analysis), but as an opportunity to discuss the actions that took place after the data breach occurred. Anthem, like other major organizations within the healthcare vertical, are members of NH-ISAC.[19] The NH-ISAC supports communication of information security between its members to give insight into and warnings about potential cyber threats within the healthcare vertical. One important initiative was the building of the National Health Cybersecurity Intelligence System. This is a healthcare-specific threat intelligence feed, leveraging STIX and TAXII (for more on the Structured Threat Information eXpression (STIX) and the Trusted Automated eXchange of Indicator Information (TAXII), refer to Chapter 5 – Knowledge Sharing and Community Support), providing automated access to security and threat intelligence, as well as alerting advisories. The knowledge elements from this data breach, identified as Indicators of Interest (IOCs), were published through this threat intelligence feed so that all NH-ISAC members could have access to them. By leveraging community sharing, the NH-ISAC was able to determine within 60 minutes the impact of the Anthem breach on its remaining members.[20] Furthermore, as these knowledge elements were now available within the NH-ISAC community, healthcare organizations could take proper steps to secure their organization's networks from similar attacks. Finally, the NH-ISAC also provided the IOCs to other ISACs within other verticals, such as the Financial Services Information Sharing and Analysis Center (FS-ISAC), to measure the larger cross-industry impact of the attack vectors used in this data breach.

[19]About Us, NHISAC, Online, http://www.nhisac.org/about-us/.

[20]The National Health ISAC (NH-ISAC) 60-Minute Response to the Anthem Attack, NH-ISAC, Online, http://www.nhisac.org/blog/the-national-health-isac-nh-isac-60-minute-response-to-the-anthem-attack/.

Target Breach Revisited

A little over a year before the Anthem data breach was front page news the retail giant Target had its own data breach. On December 15, 2013, Target discovered it was the victim of a cyber-attack that resulted in a data breach of over 70 million customer records, as well as 40 million debit and credit card account numbers. Customer records compromised as part of the data breach included:

- Names
- Mailing addresses
- Email addresses
- Phone numbers.

During a joint investigation that included a third-party incident response team, Target was able to determine that the cyberattack could be traced back several weeks to November 27, 2013. Attackers compromised one of Target's suppliers, Fazio Mechanical, using social engineering combined with Citadel, a variant of the Zeus trojan, and gained access to their credentials and to Target's supplier portals. This, based on the research performed by several different teams including the Verizon IR team, gave the attackers a place to then compromise and pivot into Target's internal networks. More can be learned about the Target breach and the potential techniques leveraged by performing a Google search for "Target data breach 2013 details" or reading articles such as *"Anatomy of the Target data breach: Missed opportunities and lessons learned"*.[21]

This data breach has been reviewed and analyzed by many different types of organizations, including security researchers and universities. Instead of revisiting the same scenarios explored in typical postmortem data breach papers including "what-ifs" and "lessons learned", we want to discuss something that was not in place at the time of this data breach, but which is now, as at the time of writing. The Retail Cyber Intelligence Sharing Center, or R-CISC, is a threat intelligence sharing community focused around the threats that target retail-based organizations.[22] It was initially founded in March 2014, several months after the public announcement of the Target breach and its impact, with more than 30 retailers initially joining the organization. R-CISC, in May 2015, formed a strategic partnership with

[21] Anatomy of the Target data breach: Missed opportunities and lessons learned, M. Kassner, ZDNet, Online, http://www.zdnet.com/article/anatomy-of-the-target-data-breach-missed-opportunities-and-lessons-learned/

[22] Retail Cyber Intelligence Sharing Center, Online, https://r-cisc.org/.

FS-ISAC to offer a real-time threat intelligence feed focused on the retail and commercial services. This community driven threat intelligence feed, like the one within NH-ISAC, provides a much needed advantage in threat modeling and threat forecasting. Target also acknowledged the value of participating within ISAC groups like these in follow-up statements 2 years after their data breach. These include comments such as "...that means sharing information about possible industry threats with other companies or through our participation in the Financial Services and Retail Information Sharing and Analysis Centers (ISACs)".[23] The R-CISC, as at the time writing, is still a very young organization. However, it will continue to grow and will hopefully bring the advantages that NH-ISAC can provide to it members.

Michaels and Staples Data Breach Analysis

We have spent some time discussing the last two data breaches in a little more detail (though not ad nauseam) than what we will discuss these final two data breaches. Though a lot of time could be focused on the analysis of the data breach, we would like to focus on the correlation between the two. Michaels, a North American arts and crafts retailer, announced on April 17, 2014 that it was in the middle of an active investigation relating to a data breach.[24] The investigation results showed that the retailer suffered two separate 8 month periods of compromise across two of its retail chains, Michaels and Aaron Brothers, and attackers were able to steal 3 million credit and debit card account numbers.[25] Another North American retailer, office supply company Staples, announced on December 19, 2014 that is was also a victim of a data breach.[26] Attackers were able to compromise the Staples network, remain within their network for up to 6 months and steal over 1 million credit card account numbers. Investigation into this data breach showed that Staples retail stores were impacted by malware that could access purchase information from customers

[23]Inside Target Corp., Days After 2013 Breach, B. Krebs., Online, http://krebsonsecurity.com/2015/09/inside-target-corp-days-after-2013-breach/.
[24]Michaels Identifies and Contains Previously Announced Data Security Issue, Business Wire, Online, http://www.businesswire.com/news/home/20140417006352/en/Michaels-Identifies-Previously-Announced-Data-Security-Issue#.U1A3P2fhf7w.
[25]3 Million Customer Credit, Debit Cards Stolen in Michaels, Aaron Brothers Breaches, B. Krebs, Online, http://krebsonsecurity.com/2014/04/3-million-customer-credit-debit-cards-stolen-in-michaels-aaron-brothers-breaches/.
[26]Staples Provides Update on Data Security Incident, Business Wire, Online, http://staples.newshq.businesswire.com/press-release/corporate/staples-provides-update-data-security-incident.

visiting up to 113 stores.[27] Research into this malware showed that it was communicating with the same command-and-control (C&C) networks as the Michaels data breach potentially linking these two compromises together and to one single attacker (or group).[28]

During our discussion of the Target data breach we highlighted a newer organization, R-CISC, that is focused on information sharing of threats targeting organizations within the retail and commercial vertical. The Michaels data breach, which was public knowledge in April 2014, could have been used to generate valuable knowledge elements in the form of IOCs and Indicators of Interest (IOIs) as well as potentially other types of knowledge elements (for a more detailed list, please refer to Chapter 4 – Identifying Knowledge Elements). Knowledge elements such as the hash value of the malicious binaries, the IP addresses of the command-and-control (C&C) servers and fingerprints of the malicious network traffic could have been leveraged by Staples to potentially thwart the attackers before their attack was successful. The Staples infrastructure has been estimated to have been compromised between April 2014 and July 2014, which is at least 2 months after the Michaels data breach compromise was confirmed to be over. If Staples was aware of the attack vectors used by the malware in the Michaels data breach, this could have potentially prevented Staples from experiencing a multi-month period in which their infrastructure had been compromised and a data breach was occurring. Community-driven threat intelligence coupled with threat forecasting powered by big data analytics may have given over 1 million Staples customers one less thing to worry about.[27] It should be noted that it is our belief, based on our research, that either Michaels did not generate knowledge elements or that Staples was not able to consume them in a usable way.

Applying Threat Forecasting Techniques

In this book we have outlined the needed tools to apply threat forecasting techniques within your organization and within this chapter we have discussed the reasons why these techniques are important. Now it is your turn (and yes we mean you!) to

[27] Staples: 6-Month Breach, 1.16 Million Cards, B. Krebs, Online, http://krebsonsecurity.com/2014/12/staples-6-month-breach-1-16-million-cards/.

[28] Link Found in Staples, Michaels Breaches, B. Krebs, Online, http://krebsonsecurity.com/2014/11/link-found-in-staples-michaels-breaches/.

begin to apply these new skills to improve your security position, as well as improve your knowledge within the threat intelligence community. The following phased approach will allow you to utilize threat forecasting in such a way that you will get the maximum benefit while improving your organization's security practices.

Phase 1—Foundational Research/Review

Phase 1 focuses on the foundational research needed to properly apply what you have learned within the preceding chapters. First, begin by examining your organization's security practices for weaknesses. An example of a weakness could be your organization's log retention policy and how log records are stored and timestamped (for accuracy in correlation of multiple logged events across multiple sources). Identifying these weaknesses may take some time, however the goal is to give these practices, including their associated policies and procedures, a thorough review. These must be implemented and adhered to before you can create the knowledge elements that you will need when performing threat modeling and, eventually, threat forecasting. While working on the review of your organization's security practices, research the threat intelligence feeds outlined in Chapter 5 (Knowledge Sharing and Community Support), as well as look for threat intelligence feeds specific to your organization's vertical. Throughout this book we have referenced real-world examples that included industry-focused threat intelligence feeds from healthcare and financial services verticals including a newly formed feed focused on retail security. The final step in phase 1 should be to review your current software tools, because some of them may already support the incorporation of threat intelligence feeds as well as the automatic creation of knowledge elements. Tools such as security information and event management solutions (SIEMs) include dashboards where the new issues found within your organization's networks can be highlighted. Once the evaluation of your existing tools is complete, you can determine if you would like to (or need to) acquire additional tools to perform threat forecasting successfully.

Phase 2—Organizational Implementation/Pattern Analysis

Phase 2 challenges you to incorporate threat intelligence into your security practices. Following the concepts in Chapter 4 (Identifying Knowledge Elements), begin to analyze and categorize the interesting data points within your organization into knowledge elements. Remember the principles discussed around signal versus noise to identify the elements that will help empower you in your threat modeling and threat forecasting. Using the concepts in Chapters 6 and 7, begin threat modeling using your knowledge elements and look for areas in which you can improve the security posture of your organization. Remember to leverage the tools at your disposal to make this as simple as possible. As mentioned in phase 1, some SIEMs may do this automatically for you. Next, using your research from phase 1, select at least one community driven threat intelligence feed and incorporate it into your threat modeling. If you are unable to get access initially to a vertical centric threat intelligence feed, begin using one of the freely available community feeds. The goal is to incorporate global knowledge into your threat modeling so that you (and your organization) can get a view of the global threat landscape and how it relates to your organization. With this knowledge, you can begin to see patterns (refer to Chapters 6 and 7) that relate to your organization's threat landscape.

Phase 3—Information Sharing/Share and Build

Phase 3 requires taking the leap discussed in Chapter 5 (Knowledge Sharing and Community Support). During phase 2 you began generating knowledge elements for use within your threat modeling. Depending on the style of knowledge elements you are creating (IOIs/IOCs/etc.), begin to contribute these knowledge elements to the threat intelligence community you joined in phase 2. The items of importance within your organization, no matter how small, may help protect another organization who has not yet discovered this knowledge element (whether or not it is active within their environment). Also, incorporate additional threat intelligence feeds. Remember that knowledge is power and more data allows for a better view at the global threat landscape. As mentioned in phase 2, you will begin to see patterns that relate to your organization's threat landscape. This is where threat forecasting will bring its power. With the help of global attack patterns, you can proactively update vulnerable operating systems or applications (such as Java or Adobe Flash). If you cannot update your environment as a protection step, you can now proactively, through predictive analysis, update security products for attacks targeting identified weaknesses. This process of analysis can be evaluated for some level of automation. This will allow you to be warned of imminent threats to your organization and allow you to take the proper action.

Now, begin threat forecasting within your organization!

Summary

The topics outlined within this chapter have connected the concepts throughout this book into a call to action. We revisited some of the major data breaches that have impacted upwards of tens of millions of customers (or subscribers in the case of Anthem) and discussed how threat forecasting should be applied in these situations to help protect other organizations within the same industry vertical or even the larger global threat intelligence community. In fact, in the Anthem data breach example we reviewed, the NH-ISAC made the knowledge elements (in the form of IOCs) available to all NH-ISAC members as well as FS-ISAC members allowing them to both determine if they have been compromised and to provide protection from these new attack vectors, which may not yet be known to their security products. We reviewed historical threat reporting, discussed how it is not a replacement for threat forecasting and outlined how it compliments threat forecasting. The values of historical threat reporting cannot be ignored, however the pitfalls, specifically around the staleness of data related to today's threat landscape, are addressed by a properly implemented threat modeling and threat forecasting process. Finally, a three-phased approach to entering threat forecasting was provided to help lower the barrier for entry and make this new technique more accessible. Successful implementation of threat forecasting techniques, powered by big data, will give you the data you need to better understand your organization's threat landscape and give you actionable intelligence so that your organization can help prevent it from being the next major data breach.

10

THE ROAD AHEAD

Synopsis

In this following chapter, each of the authors will provide their insights, challenges and opinions on the future of security and threat forecasting. The authors combined have several decades of experience in security and extremely diverse backgrounds in product development, consulting, research and engineering to name a few. They all have had the honor of traveling the world with opportunities to consult, strategize and speak on various security topics with governments and some of the largest companies in the world. This collective experience has provided the basis and idea for this book. As you can imagine, John Pirc, David DeSanto, Iain Davidson, and Will Gragido, all great friends working for different security organizations, provide their unfiltered assessment of what the road ahead holds for security. You'll find that, while there was violent agreement on general themes, in some cases there was friendly and respectful disagreement on specifics.

John Pirc

I embarked on this project, threat forecasting, almost 4 years ago while traveling to Prague when I came up with the idea. However, I was in the final stages of finishing my second book and shelved the idea for about a year, for, as you can image, the research involved in writing a book is no trivial task. It requires a lot of commitment and the ability to pull together incredibly smart minds that believe in your initial idea and embrace it, and are capable of molding it. I was extremely fortunate to have David DeSanto, Iain Davidson, and Will Gragido join the project as one unified team throughout its course. In working for some of the largest security vendors in the world in product management, engineering, strategy and research, you are exposed to a

Threat Forecasting. http://dx.doi.org/10.1016/B978-0-12-800006-9.00010-0

lot of interesting ideas and if those ideas don't lead to revenue, well it's just a great idea. Innovation within any established vendor organization is risky, especially when your ideas are little radical and fall outwith what is considered the norm. This is completely understandable, but Steve Jobs was correct in saying, "You have to do things differently…" and that "…everything in what we call life was made up by people no smarter than you and me." Sometimes you have to place it all on the line and risk everything. The concept of threat forecasting to the execution of threat forecasting is not going to be a trivial task and some will think it is impossible, but in order to solve large complex problems you have to think big without worrying about what other people will say and do. Trust me, in publishing two books, doing press and publishing research…you learn to have a thick skin. I've learned you can't please everyone, but at the very least this book demonstrates the possibilities of how threat forecasting can make a difference.

When I look into the future of cyber security, all the advancements in technology from smart devices, (phones, tablets, wearables, drones, Internet of Things (IoT), etc.) to new coding languages are only going to complicate our ability to reduce risk. This is not going to be easy, but as technologists we need to stay ahead of that curve. To further complicate the issue we have to deal with encryption both in transit and at rest. I've written a paper on SSL decryption and what I can say is that it has been and will continue to be the Achilles heel for gaining insight into data without breaking down the integrity and confidentially of the data we are inspecting for malicious active and threats.

There has also been movement around the world pushing for backdoors in vendor platforms and software. I'm not going to get in the debate of what's right or wrong from a political stand point, but I will state my opinion from a technologist stand point. In my entire career of making security products, I was never once asked to share our code base or even asked to add a requirement that would allow a third party access to my products. I know with all the press around Snowden and the NSA, I constantly hear that this was being done. Thank goodness, none of the companies I worked for had any problem in providing anyone access. When you are selling a security product worldwide with \$500 million–\$1 billion in annual revenues…well giving said access would severely limit your ability to sell and compete in the global market place. In working with and for some of the largest and well-known security researchers in the world that hunt for vulnerabilities in code, platforms and backdoors…all I can say is that the things they have found and that I've witnessed firsthand…well, they are simply amazing. I say this because if good guys place a backdoor in any product and it's likely a product that has a lot of market share, someone will eventually find it and this will open a whole can of worms in providing a jump point for hackers. I completely understand the spirit in which this is suggested, as terrorist organizations and other people with nefarious intentions are hiding behind encryption. I just bring this topic up because if we progress in this direction it will further complicate our ability to ensure the confidentially and integrity of data and communications.

Lastly, I think we are certainly passed what I call carpet bombing threats for the sake of disseminating a broad-based attack across multiple industry verticals and waiting for what you get back. The focus on industry vertical attacks has and will continue to grow towards becoming the norm in terms of targets from the adversary. We have seen this in the past few years and certainly talked about the various retail vendors getting breached throughout this entire book. Personal, identifiable information and credit card data are still valuable targets, but that information doesn't compare to the personal, identifiable information a hacker can get from a mortgage banking company and even information from healthcare organizations. One would think that this type of information would be encrypted, but, according to some breach statistics I heard at a recent security talk, in all of the breaches in 2014, only 4% of the data stolen was encrypted. Playing armchair quarterback, this seems like an easy fix and there are plenty of products that provide the ability to encrypt data at rest. However, encrypting multiple databases is not a trivial task, as I've learnt from asking multiple Chief Security Officers who absolutely want to do this, but the implementation is costly and sometimes can be too complex depending on their environment. In going forward, I don't think the future of security looks bleak, despite some of my comments above, but we need to continue and push the limits in coming up with new threat detection and prevention techniques.

David DeSanto

I will first say that it is quite fun to be writing "the road ahead" and providing predictions after beating you over the head chapter after chapter with direction on using data analytics to predict your next steps. That said, this is where you can find the principles of looking at historical data and current trends as historical threat reports do, as discussed in Chapters 1 and 9, and begin to follow the patterns to see where the future may take us.

This book has been focused on the power that comes with properly using threat intelligence, especially when coupled with techniques like threat modeling. Several years ago threat intelligence data was something for us researchers to play around with, build threat models and capture malicious objects to analyze. This is slowly becoming less and less the case, as the Information Sharing and Analysis Centers (ISACs) are building their own dedicated threat intelligence feeds focused on threats targeting their industry verticals. Furthermore, new startups are appearing that are focused solely on threat intelligence and are offering products/services that offer assistance with time to detection and highlight issues within your organization's infrastructure. This trend is going to continue over the next 5–10 years as more traditional security product vendors begin to push more into the threat intelligence space (not from a pure research perspective, but from a product offering perspective). This will lead to some of the concepts within this book becoming as common as today's traditional network firewall. IT organizations will begin their days looking at threat intelligence dashboards outlining new threat scenarios and impacts to their threat landscapes versus the current traditional IT day of looking at log events and system update data. This will eventually include "virtual patching" of the infrastructure allowing IT organizations to selectively apply custom signatures or policies to security products based on knowledge elements received via threat intelligence feeds. This fundamental shift in the paradigm for IT will help reduce the time to detection of a data breach and hopefully lower the volume of data breaches occurring today.

Encryption is the devil! (No, not really.) Like John, I believe that encryption is going to continue to be a major issue for the information security industry and governments around the world for as long as we, as the people of the world, continue to try to protect the world from people with evil intentions. Whether you look at some of the arguments over the past decade or so, or look into the arguments of today, the recurring theme is that encryption is giving "the enemy," which currently has the face of terrorism, a leg up and is letting them "win." Following this recurring theme governments are asking security product vendors to provide them with their private encryption keys, as well as to put backdoors into their products to facilitate easier "sniffing" or listening to communications. Over the next 5 years more regulations will be imposed onto industry verticals and, consequently, the information security industry. These will include a combination of higher cryptographic standards, as we are seeing with the birth of HTTP/2 and its requirements as outlined in RFC 7540.[1] This recurring theme is not going to go away and we, within the boarder information technology community (including information security), need to find a way to support the initiatives without compromising the principles of privacy and rendering encryption pointless.

[1] Hypertext Transfer Protocol Version 2 (HTTP/2), M. Belshe, IETF, Online, https://tools.ietf.org/html/rfc7540

The last area I want to focus on is the push of data to the cloud. More people and organizations are pushing sensitive data to the Internet, including personal data, intellectual property (including source code) and customer data. We will see a shift in the targets for data breaches from large retailers to the companies that are offering these services for large enterprises and organizations within almost every industry vertical. Furthermore, there is an insurgence of companies specializing in single sign-on functionality linking all of your enterprise apps to one single two-factor authenticated account within their products/services. These companies will also become the new favorite target for data breaches, as they are the gateway to a treasure trove of data. We as consumers of the Internet need to decide at what point ease of access is too much and security needs to become a priority (again). This is well highlighted in a funny yet fitting commercial Microsoft had for Windows 7 and "the cloud." This commercial featured two people stranded at an airport. Bored with the delay at the airport, they hop onto the airport wireless (which was most likely someone spoofing the wireless network, however we will skip that security flaw for a moment) to connect to their home TV recordings to entertain themselves. Once they access their videos, the woman proclaims "Yay! Cloud!" at the ability to now watch TV. These interconnected services, including social media like Facebook and LinkedIn, hold sensitive information including credit card information. The security of the cloud is very foggy right now and needs extra attention in the coming years if we do not want this to become the undiscovered country of data breaches.

There is no cloud

it's just someone else's computer

The final thought I want to leave you with is time. Time to detection and time to patch are going to become more critical as we move forward in the information technology age. Most of the data breach use cases we reviewed in this book took months to detect from the initial compromise of the infrastructure, and it also took time, in some cases, to patch the vulnerabilities exploited as part of the data breach. The time elapses in both cases need to be shortened to as close to real-time as possible if we are going to secure our data as best as possible. Combine the threat intelligence and threat forecasting principles discussed in this book and make knowledge elements available in near real-time and we can increase the level of difficulty for compromising our networks.

Iain Davison

While this project has been eye opening and it has been an honor to be able to work on it, the forecast that the doom and gloom of the dark web will seep out from the shadows and compromised us all, would just be a little too easy to believe. For the most part there are already articles and forums scaring people to lock away their credit card and buckle down, as this is going to be yet another harrowing year of corruption, fraud and identity theft. It's what they don't tell you that is the truly scary part of all of this.

The number of breaches will continue to grow, with more and more individual's data being stolen. There will clearly be an escalation point moving from the now low hanging fruit of credit card fraud to larger targets of health records, as this information costs a lot more on the market places of the dark web.

As for the ability to forecast these breaches, it will be a slow path as many companies do not want to share or disclose breaches with/to industry peers in the name of competition or because they might also be a publically traded company and sharing this kind of information cause their stock price to drop. This is one of the reasons why malicious actors are winning in the constant battle to protect corporate and government information. Too many bad companies are making money out of being part of the problem and not part of the solution. Many security vendors are more interested in jamming an entire suite of their product down the prospective customer's throats without thinking if it's really going to help protect them against a malicious actor.

Raising the budgets for companies to start protecting their assets and intellectual property is something that also needs to happen and fast. Sadly, what many of the companies are focusing on is one box to cover all the bases. So they only have to make a single purchase and tick the box, as it's easier to manage and they won't have to spend money on more employees to keep up with the day-to-day operations of the security appliances.

To add to the long list of breaches that are sure to happen this year, as more and more companies are compromised and customer data is exfiltrated, no company is looking forward as to how they are going to proactively protect themselves or make themselves aware of what is going in the wild. It's wise to study the ways of your adversary.

Will Gragido

I was asked to join this project to help its founder, John Pirc, and the other co-authors, David DeSanto and Iain Davison, realize their collective vision with respect to threat forecasting and prediction while adding my own unique perspective and ideas to the project in order to further enhance the outcome. I always find questions related to threat forecasting and prediction challenging. I'm reminded of what Ray Bradbury said when he was asked if he was predicting the future in his work. Bradbury said "I was not predicting the future, I was trying to prevent it." Now, if you know anything about Bradbury's work you'll know that some of it, particularly works such as Fahrenheit 451, paints a dyspotic society; a society or community that is undesirable or frightening. This is also the case with questions related to the future as it is influenced and driven by threat forecasting and prediction. The truth is that as an industry we have more data related to cyber threat intelligence than we can put to good use. That said, there is a remarkable volume of threat intelligence data that are valuable for a fleeting moment and, then, like a star experiencing its last nuclear reaction prior to going cold, it fades. Threat forecasting and prediction is not something that can or should be approached casually when one's intent is to truly and accurately predict a state that will empower a defender to defend his or her network from a well versed and experienced adversary. As a result, many things must be considered:

1. The source(s) of the threat intelligence being used in the forecasting and prediction:
   a. Open source intelligence (OSINT)
   b. Closed/private source intelligence
   c. Machine oriented intelligence
   d. HUMINT derived intelligence
   e. Human analyst—cyber threat intelligence interaction and balance

2. The credibility of the source(s) being used in the forecasting and prediction modeling
3. The accuracy of the source(s) and the data they are providing
4. The quality of the data they are providing
5. The infrastructure to accommodate disparate sources of data
6. The ability of this infrastructure to collect, aggregate, normalize, and analyze the threat intelligence
7. The ability to integrate both system and human intelligence into a platform or system that can be easily mined and used for the express purpose of developing data relationships and linkages between artifacts, operations, campaigns, and adversaries
8. The ability to take all of the data that are available to you, verify their applicability, and then act accordingly.

So now onto some predictions:

1. In order for anyone to properly forecast threats or predict them, they must reduce the signal to noise ratio. So what does that mean? That means that for an analyst he or she must work with those parties who administer their backend system so that it may be optimized and enabled to jettison non-important or inapplicable data. This can only happen if there is a fundamental shift in thought and deed with respect to how cyber threat intelligence is collected, handled, analyzed, and applied.
2. Individuals and teams will need to be able to sell the idea and concept within their organizations so that they may gain the greatest amount of support for the initiative(s) possible.
3. Individuals and enterprises will need to question the threat intelligence data they receive from third parties while establishing their own sources.
4. Individuals and enterprises will need to investigate their own privately sourced data with a high degree of scrutiny.
5. Adversarial analysis will become absolutely integral to the collection, aggregation, normalization, and analysis of data (proprietary or otherwise); so knowing one's enemy will become of paramount importance.
6. There must be recognition that the numbers of cyber crimes and cyber criminals will continue to grow and that these criminals will mature their efforts by taking advantage of technologies such as the Dark Web to obfuscate their movements
7. There must be recognition that in light of #6, more and more cyber criminal activity will take place in the Surface Web and Deep Web.
8. Finally, in recognition of #7, a great degree of data science experience and expertise will be required in the enterprise and non-enterprise shops (read: vendors).

Threat forecasting and prediction will only occur by coupling the art and sciences of traditional intelligence analysis and cyber threat intelligence analysis in concert with big data analytics. It is my hope as a practitioner and author that we will see this become a reality for more and more organizations on a global basis.

Summary

The future of cyber security is complex and will no doubt be made even more complicated by the advancements in technology that the world is experiencing on an almost daily basis: technologies such as smart phones, tablets, wearables (e.g., "fitbit", Apple Watch), drones, IoT, etc. All of these devices will—at one point in time or another—become sources for data that can be used in big data analytics activities that aid in promoting threat forecasting and predictive analysis. Other trends, such as those associated with the adoption of encryption and cloud-based technologies, will influence and introduce new challenges to those seeking to conduct threat forecasting and predictive analysis. In order to glean as much from the environments called out above, the following steps must be followed:

- The security data being collected from these environments (e.g., knowledge elements—IOA, IOC, IOI, etc.) must be pure and irrefutable.
- The combination of machine oriented data and human analytics will come together and build from the successes of any big data system.
- The sources associated with these environments must be credible and, as such, all efforts to collect security and threat intelligence for the express purpose of developing threat forecasting data must rely on credible data sources and data.
- The reduction of the "signal"-"noise" ratio is integral to the process of properly integrating threat intelligence data into the big data analytics environments.
- The development of a repetitious cycle is carried out and embraced as part of an enterprise or research organizations tasks.

INDEX

Note: Page numbers followed by "*f*" indicate figures, "*t*" indicate tables, and "*b*" indicate boxes.

Printed in the United States
By Bookmasters